THE
CENTURY
SPEAKS

HEREFORDSHIRE
voices

School nativity play, 1946.

THE
CENTURY
SPEAKS

HEREFORDSHIRE
voices

Memories of Herefordshire people
compiled by Genevieve Tudor from interviews by Julia Letts and Sue Broome
for the **BBC Hereford and Worcester** *series*
The Century Speaks

TEMPUS

First published 1999
Copyright © BBC Hereford and Worcester, 1999

Tempus Publishing Limited
The Mill, Brimscombe Port,
Stroud, Gloucestershire, GL5 2QG

ISBN 0 7524 1838 6

Typesetting and origination by
Tempus Publishing Limited
Printed in Great Britain by
Midway Clark Printing, Wiltshire

CONTENTS

Alvis Evans with her brother and parents in 1932.

Mostyn Street and Greenland Road's end-of-war street party, 1945.

FOREWORD

This is my chance to say a huge thank you to all those who agreed to tell me their stories for *The Century Speaks*. It took me the best part of six months to record the interviews (many of which are reproduced in this book) and every minute of it was a privilege and a pleasure.

Each interview has been unique. On one occasion, I arrived in north-west Herefordshire expecting to talk to a farmer of 103, and ended up interviewing his son, grandson and great-grandson as well. On another occasion, I interviewed a woman scanning her sheep on a beautiful snowy morning on the hills above Dorstone – a sight I will never forget. Two of my interviews took place in Herefordshire castles, one in a gypsy wagon and one in a cowshed. I've discovered corners of Herefordshire that I didn't know existed and I've gained an extraordinary insight into the lives of about a hundred Herefordians.

Roy Conod helps with the haymaking, 1940s.

I've been amazed by the clarity of people's memories and their honesty, often telling me things that they've never told anyone before. I've cried with several interviewees, and laughed with many of them. And I can truthfully say that not once have I been bored.

Inevitably, in making the radio programmes and compiling this book, we've had to leave tons of material out. This is just a snapshot of the century. If you want the full picture, then go to the British Library and immerse yourself in oral history for a day. Every word we recorded is now part of a new sound archive, 'The Millennium Memory Bank'.

If I have learnt anything from the wonderful Herefordshire people who have shared their lives with me during this project, it is that we should all do more listening. We should find more time to question and share the experiences of our parents and grandparents, friends and neighbours. Think what a waste it is if we don't.

Julia Letts
Producer, *The Century Speaks*

CHAPTER 1
Where we live

'Claston', 1919.

Fairs and hot cross buns, hop picking and escapologist porkers, close-knit communities and Celtic settlements … Herefordshire has it all. Both 'incomers' and Herefordians talk about the county in which they live:

Caius Hawkins loves both Herefordshire and the people who live here:

Geographically, it's wonderful. You've got the mountains – well, I suppose they are more like big hills – and you've got the River Wye which is very beautiful and you've got the edge of England. It's also a place that has been forgotten about in many respects. There's still people that have lived here all their lives and so there is still some of the rural community left here. There's also historical stuff, being border country. There's also quite a lot of interesting people moved into the county. I mean, hidden away round here are some fascinating people, in terms of artists and creative people. There is quite an intellectual side to this area too.

Caius Hawkins, born 1965

Alvis Evans described the county town and the fairs:

Hereford was small. It sort of encompassed one, like a car does. You felt at home in it. It was after the war when it really started to increase. Then it wasn't quite so good. Even as a child, though, there were 'no go' areas. You didn't go down to Hunterton because there were some slums in Catherine Street and they built a new housing estate and they moved them all out of Catherine Street to Hunterton – so they moved a ghetto out of town. We did not go down there. They were rougher than us. I like to think of myself as a country person. When we moved to Ross Road there were very few houses and we were always out in the fields. We used to save our pennies all year round for the May fairs. We'd walk right up to the railway station and the fair started in the station grounds. All the way down Commercial Road, Union Street, St Peter's Square, Commercial Street, High Town, Eign Street, Broad Street, King Street and it ended with the Wall of Death opposite Bridge Street, and the Helter Skelter which was right outside our house. By the time we'd finished we were worn out. They always had the naughty shows, you know, the dancing girls, which I used to find absolutely fascinating, right outside the Methodist church in Commercial Road! It was a wonderful gay time. That fair was granted a Royal Charter hundreds of years ago and all the money goes to the cathedral – or it did then. It was the entertainment of the year. This fair lasted three days and it was full of revelry. There was nobody standing up and being sold for labour, which is what all fairs were about in the first place. Everybody loved that fair and everybody was out. The only other time you'd see everybody out was New Year's Eve. And you did dance in the street on New Year's Eve. All the church bells rang, all the trains hooted and everybody laughed and sang and danced the New Year in. You don't see that now. On Good Friday you'd have the man walk round with a great big tray of steaming hot cross buns on his head. You used to lean out of your bedroom windows and pick the buns off his tray and put your money in.

Alvis Evans, born 1927

Roy Conod describes the country idyll:

I used to love going up the old coaching lane from our house. I used to walk up there and sit on the huge bank, which had been part of [the] stone quarry, and watch the foxes go in and out and play with their young ones and the badgers and rabbits, and go up there to the bluebell woods and pick bluebells and take them home to my mother. Life was idyllic in a way and I don't think that's rose-coloured spectacles I'm looking through. It was very much like that. I should say the main change has been brought about by farming itself. The need to make farms larger to accommodate the mechanisation. Hedges went and, walking up the road here, I can see there are huge fields on either side of me which would be many fields. Just recently, one of the things that has changed it is you see fewer cattle in the fields. When I came here the people that bought the local farm had pedigree Herefords. We hardly ever see any Herefords in Herefordshire anymore, unless they are in some show.

Roy Conod, born 1938

My first impression of Hereford was I was going to love it forever. I stepped off the railway station on a glorious day on 15th October 1942 – I was seventeen. I'd come to do my bit in the Women's Timber Corp. We were greeted by four girls [on a lorry] and that was the only time I had the luxury of sitting in the cab. [After that] I was on the back of the lorry in all sorts of weather! I was taken to a milk bar in Hereford and bought a milk shake and I thought, 'This is the life for me. I'm going to enjoy this.' Hereford itself was a sleepy little market town. Everything about it was tranquil. We soon learned all about the Black Mountains and the Malvern Hills and some of the history of Hereford – how Nell Gwyn had lived here, and all about John Garrick and the theatre and the lovely cathedral with the one and only chained library. I remember being shown the place where Nell Gwyn was born – it had a plaque. It was nostalgic. It had a lovely river, it had tennis courts, it offered all the pursuits anyone could want.

Joan Thomas, born 1925

The local community has changed over the century. There are contrasting views from Herefordians:

I've never really made friends with neighbours, certainly in this village. Everybody keeps to themselves, it's very quiet. There's not a community spirit, here, anyway. We say 'hello' to next door. We're polite and we'll chat across the fence and they'll take post in for us if a parcel comes but we've not said 'Come round for coffee, have a chat,' partly because I just don't want to (which sounds bizarre but it's quite nice the way it is). I was chatting with a friend not all that long ago about communities and I just perceive my community as all the friends I know, dotted all over the place,

The Haven, Hardwicke.

rather than being where I live. It's my friends, not here.

Helen Winterbotham-Pope, born 1972

I think it is a closeness and a familiarity which has two sides to it. The closeness that can be really positive – other friendships that you build up and the knowledge the you have of your peer group – and it's not just a knowledge that you have of them, but its a knowledge of their family, their background and you know an awful lot about these people. One, because you've known them so long, and two, because the kind of environment in which you live means your parents probably know them and maybe other families' grandparents knew your grandparents or whatever. There's a real history of familiarity. But the reverse of that is desperately suffocating – or can be. Everybody knows absolutely everything about your business and I, personally, was so relieved to go to university and move out of those circles and meet people who didn't know the dodgy haircut I had when I was thirteen, or didn't know that I'd been out with the awful boy when I was twelve. All those kind of silly things, but also the more serious things as well. From my experiences of living in London, the anonymity can be equally as disconcerting because you don't know anybody. That's quite strange coming from my background but at the same time there is a part of me that finds it desperately refreshing.

Emma Moore

I found it very easy [to become part of the community]. There's a friendly pub in the village, I like going down there and they are quite a jolly crowd. They have a quiz on a Thursday night, and a little gang of us who like playing chess, we gather there on a Monday night. I got to know most of the villagers here … it's a very friendly village. They'll do pretty well anything for you. They are a good-hearted crowd of people. [There have been changes here,] the view from my bedroom window used to be hop fields – hop farming is going through a bit of a crisis. One or two of the hop farmers in the area are able to survive by modernising and growing new varieties of hops, these dwarf hops, that are easier to harvest. They don't need so many pickers, less labour intensive than the old hop farming, but there are some hop farmers down here who have actually got out of the business, so the landscape from my window, instead of hop fields is now a whole sea of rape and barley and other things growing in the fields down there. I'm sad to see the demise of the hop – especially as I'm fond of beer – I like real ales which need good quality Hereford hops which have got a good nose on them but I don't feel terribly sentimental about it. I suppose it had to happen.

Harry Pugh, born 1934

At first it was quite hard to find the community because this is known as Hardwicke but I think it's technically known as a 'scattered Celtic settlement'. We're on the B-road and about a quarter of a mile away is the church, and a third of a mile away is the pub and the school is the same distance in the other direction, then it's just a few farms. It was difficult to find the village and one of the

Roy Conod and a family group, 1940s.

Bushelling hops at Claston.

things I missed enormously was people walking past. No one walked by. Occasionally there were cattle being driven past and cars but no one to give a friendly wave. So it really meant making an effort to find the people there. Mind you, the first few days we were here, we realised there was a community and people were interested. We went down to a pub for a meal and while we were there, [there] were a couple of ladies one side of the log fire and a couple the other side and we were at the bar and were talking and we suddenly heard them say, 'Have you seen the new people at the Haven yet?' and the others said, 'No, but there was a light on last night so they must be there' and at that point we introduced ourselves because we thought things might be said they'd regret later on! But there was obviously an interest … they were very friendly here … perhaps borders make for change and

they are used to having people moving between areas. We have found some of the ways of the local Herefordians a bit different and we've laughed a bit – but I'm quite sure they've laughed at our obsession with dates and diaries. I think it's affectionate laughter. I think we've been very lucky in Hardwicke – the mix of incomers to locals – and the incomers have not thrown their weight about too much. They want to help but they haven't tried to take over.

Janet Robinson, born 1935

There was great community spirit in those days because at that time there was no electricity, no proper radio – I can remember the Cat's Whisker period going right through to bringing the wet acid batteries back from Leominster to have for the radio. Therefore, the

14

community life was thriving. The village hall was an old tin shed but it was well used. We had visiting performers, plays, even circuses come there. I'll never forget going to the circus and seeing the clowns and small animals performing in the village hall and then going round to a local farmer and seeing the cages with bears and lions and monkeys in them – things that we'd never seen before so it was quite exciting. The village hall was used for everything, from whist drives to regular dances, harvest suppers, local talent competitions, and concerts. It was the centre of the community like the church was. It brought the whole community together and the community worked together and we all knew each other very well because of that.

Roy Conod, born 1938

Ann Jenkins was born and brought up in the village of Orleton. She talks about the changes that have taken place there:

There were orchards and patches of land in between, which have all been built on. [It made me sad at first] but we've had such nice people come into the village who helped so much with everything. There's lots of new people that have helped so much I don't mind now. At the beginning I didn't like it much. I used to think, 'It's our village and they are all coming in'. But I think you've got to have a mix if your village is going to keep going. It's got to grow otherwise villages die out. [Some villages] have lost their post office, their shop, their school. Some of them have even lost their church. They haven't got the facilities Orleton has got. We've got a doctor and a bakery and the bus comes

The Haven, Hardwicke near Hay-on-Wye.

through the village. We seem to have got most of the amenities we need. I walk down to the shop perhaps two or three times a week. It's the post office and shop and they've got nearly everything you want, and if they haven't got it they'll get it for you. I walk the dog in the morning so I meet people then. I'm always walking about the village. Everybody talks to you and if you don't know them you say, 'Good afternoon' and you think, 'I wonder where they are from and what they are doing'. Holidaymakers, we always put it down to. People are very helpful to each other. You know when you talk to people they say, 'We live in the best part of the village!' and you think, 'Well, you can't because we live in the best part of the village!' and then you talk to somebody else and they say, 'We've got a real little community down our way'.

Ann Jenkins, born 1939

Gary Starkey describes sunrise above the Dorstone farm:

The trees were all silhouetted behind this beautiful sky, and it spread right across like a mackerel sky and the sheep were silhouetted and it was so still, it was beautiful. We all stood and watched it. People spend masses of money on fireworks but no one can repeat that sort of thing, you just can't do it. [The sunset,] the trees, the shapes are beautiful, especially when they are naked, against the snow.

You can see seven counties from the top and at night, if it's really clear, you can see clusters of lights where the towns are and in the morning the sunrise is spectacular.

I'm standing about 1,200-foot up, under a hill under the Black Mountains by the Kevin Hill You can look down across Hereford, out towards Gloucester, Leominster and back out towards the Clee Hills. I love it up here. It's bracing and it's free and it's open. We are probably the highest farm in the area. BT wanted to put a mast on our land. They said there's no interference between here and the Urals in Russia. We said if they came in the winter we could tell them [that] without any expensive equipment!

We don't have as much snow as we used to have but I can certainly remember, with the children, walking from hedge top to hedge top and we couldn't keep any of the animals in because they'd just walk over the top of the gates. We were cut off for three weeks in 1970-something – the army came to get us out and it was spectacular. They came in with their snow blowers and they opened all the roads up and they couldn't believe we were still snowed in when everyone on the bottom was chugging around quite normally!

Gary Starkey, born 1951

I think the thing we loved as children was to be able to go up over the hill and look down into Woolhope, and we loved that and I think we loved the fact that you didn't have to go very far and you'd got a fresh view. That first spring, I can remember the apple blossom, how beautiful it was, and taking a whole branch off a tree into my mother and having it explained to me that I couldn't pick a branch off a tree because those were Mr Thompson's apples I was picking! But I think apple blossom time, even now, is one of my favourite times because it reminds me of when we first came here.

Jill Southall, born 1938

Hop farmer Peter Davies remembers the old days:

Hop picking in the olden days … was the highlight of the year. There was tremendous preparation because we had people living on the farm. They used to sleep in the stable and in the loft above the stable and in one of the cattle sheds. There used to be special trains bringing hop pickers to Claston and we used to go to meet them with a wagon or car to bring the luggage. It was something you looked forward to, and when hop picking ceased and they all disappeared it was quite dreadful really, because the kilns work twenty-four hours a day except Sundays and the whole place was alive with people and activity and noise and smells. Something that I will never forget [is] the friendliness and the comradeship with the Welsh people and the local people.

Peter Davies, born 1923

Doris Tunley remembers hop picking in the holidays:

We used to love hop picking. My mother called it a holiday. You didn't go to school because school holidays was worked in with the hop picking. We would go off in the morning down to the hop fields and it would be all wet and dewy and there were houses (as they was called) with so many binds would be in it and you picked that house out and you didn't interfere with the one next door to you – you didn't take their hops. So if you had a poor batch of hops you got on with it but next time they tried to put you into a better lot of hops,

Peter Davies and his sister, Claston, *c.* 1930.

17

and gradually as you cleared them the hop yard would be just wires and strings hanging up. The daughter of the farm used to come with a big basket and weigh them up – the man did stand at the end with the crib – the crib was made with wood and canvas, and then as she tipped one in he'd shout 'One' and she'd fill another and he'd shout 'Two' and sometimes you'd get eight and sometimes ten and you'd listen to see what the others had got and you'd say, 'Oh, they've done well, haven't they?'

Doris Tunley, born 1924

I think of all the jobs done on the farm, bushelling was my favourite because you met all the people and by the end of the month you got to know them quite well. The first day I did the bushelling and there was another busheller as well, because it was more than one could do, [and he] said to me that if you have a problem with a person and she grumbles a lot [you should] say, 'Fair enough, I accept that I haven't done it right'. And you'd tip the hops out of the sack (you used to put eight bushels in the sack) into her crib, give her the basket and tell her to do it and she will never get them as much as you do because once the hops have been bushelled they are flattened and you get more in the basket and I did this to a very quarrelsome lady. She had a lot of hops, she was a very good picker and from memory she made them about two bushels less than I had so I never had another squabble. They did have reason to grumble sometimes and it was a horrible job if it was wet, but the skilled hop pickers would pick all day without getting wet. They had their large

umbrella and their thick leather apron and they would sit on the side of the crib with their back to the rain and pick happily all day long and they would not be wet by the end of the day.

Peter Davies, born 1923

A contrasting view, but there was sometimes a downside!

If the weather was lovely it was gorgeous, but if it was wet it was horrible and if you'd got a bind come across your neck they were ever so rough and they wouldn't half rag you. Your neck would be sore. Your hands would get black, and you couldn't get it off but the best thing to do was to take the big [hop] leaves. They were very big leaves, like a big oak leaf, and take some of them home with you and just damp them and rub them in your hands and that would clean it off … but your hands got very dirty and rough. You could leave things under your crib and mum used to take a big knife and you'd cut the bind off at the bottom. [The foreman] didn't like us doing those. He reckoned it was bad for them and yet now they cut them all down and take them in to pick, don't they? There's no hop picking now. And I think it got people together. They had a good time and the kids would go round scrumping and it was a wonderful life.

Doris Tunley, born 1924

18

Hop picking with Doris Tunley's family.

John Thacker describes the Red Cross sale in Bromyard which led to the escaped pig on the downs:

During the war they had sales in Bromyard and all the farmers gave something to the auction then … perhaps they gave one sheep or a pig, or a small calf or some potatoes and it was all auctioned and the farmers bought it but all the money went to the Red Cross for the war effort – and the boss went down to this Red Cross sale and he wanted to buy something and he bought a little pig. One little pig. And he put it in his trailer behind his car and then he stopped and had a drink or two in Bromyard and came back to the farm and he looked in the trailer and of course

there was no pig. He'd jumped out on the way home! So in the morning he said, 'John, I want you to get on your bike and go and look for this pig' and I thought I'd never find this pig. Anyway I got on my bike and got as far as Bromyard Downs and I looked across all these acres of bracken and bushes and [I thought] 'If ever the pig's in there I shall never, ever find him'. I thought it's not worth just looking under these bushes, you'd wouldn't know where he was. So I came home … and there was a little post office, Tedstone Wafre Post Office and there was a lady in there and I asked her if she'd seen a little pig and she *had* seen the little pig, in the field opposite on the corner and there was an old barn across there and [we] went across and … this pig was asleep in the manger in this barn. We caught him and put him in the trailer and took him home and I thought I was lucky to find that pig! But that cattle shed now, where we found the pig, is a luxurious home, a beautiful house now. In fact I had a drink down there only last year and I often think when I'm sat in this posh sitting room about catching this pig under the manger there! Things were so different in those days. You had more time.

John Thacker, born 1927

Ledbury is becoming much more a tourist town instead of a market town than it once was. I think it's losing the character that it had but I think everywhere is. I think the culture of Ledbury is changing. I do find it's quite funny when people say it's such a lovely town, it's so pretty and calm and tranquil – and it is but I think, like a lot of small market towns in the area where we live, it has a lot of underlying tensions and a lot of underlying problems that aren't really seen. A lot of the houses that have been built, I personally think, are really out of character with the whole town. There's been attempts made, I mean they are red brick 'samey' houses, built on little cul-de-sacs, and there is an attempt made to keep them in with the Tudor facade of the houses that are very old in Ledbury – but they are so close together, and they are so modern in their outlook, I just find it quite sad. And they're built so quickly. Of course, I'm not saying new people shouldn't come to the area. I feel so privileged to have been brought up here – it would be terrible to suggest other people shouldn't have that

advantage. But just the way it's done. I don't think it's been particularly well thought out.

Emma Moore

I would never leave Ross. Ross is my home. It's the longest place I've stayed for one time in my life. I've been here thirty years – it's a very beautiful part of the country. I love it immensely, the people are warm, you're living on the borders of Hereford and Wales and both Herefordians and Welsh have that lovely warmth. I can't think of anywhere else I would want to bring up my children, which I have done, my grandchildren and hopefully my great-grandchildren. When we came here, Brookend Street and Broad Street were desolate, most shops were closed down, they were tatty and one by one they all folded. We were able to buy property in Brookend Street … and it's a more communal area … so that part of the town is up and coming. It's come up and I think the icing on the cake was when they opened the post office in the Maltings.

Jackie Danter, born 1944

I look back on Ross as though I dreamt it. But I think it really was like that. We lived by the church which had a very famous area called the Prospect which overlooks the bend in the River Wye. And I had so many happy picnics in the Prospect with my brother and mum and dad, and playing cricket and, just further up the street where we lived, was a putting green and a tennis court – many a happy summer was spent there.

Everywhere was on my doorstep. But prettiness was what I remember.

Lynne Hunter, born 1959

Dave Morris welcomes incomers to his village of Luston:

I think it's very good that we've built and we've got people out in the country. I know you get the odd one that comes from London and thinks there shouldn't be a dog barking or that the cock shouldn't crow in the morning. They've mostly fitted in, but the one thing I don't like about them is now they don't want nobody else to build and have a house, which seems funny to me. The people that come in are generally retired people – so they've gone on all the local councils, which were before their time run by the likes of myself and my grandfather and we'd say, 'Tom wants a house, we better let him have planning permission to put one there for his boy'. And that's how it went on … 'they want 100 council houses?' 'Yes, that's alright. Let the people from Leominster … let them come and live in Luston'. When I was on the Parish Council, that was the way I viewed it, but I went off three years ago because I got fed up of the people that had come in not wanting change, whereas we'd allowed the change for them to come in. How are they protecting the countryside when they're driving the young people away from it? We're going to end up with the villages full of people like grandfather, 103. Well, who's going to look after him?

Dave Morris, born 1953

When the first grandchild was born I actually took that child, aged three, for a walk in the snow around Kington. I described all the footprints in the snow – foxes and badgers and all that sort of thing. And after about an hour I took him back and his grandmother asked, 'What have you been doing?' 'Grandfather has been showing me tracks in the snow' and she said, 'What tracks?' and he said, 'Hippopotamus, elephants … ' But the point is they walked, they went out. I'm disappointed that even they, in this area, are not so aware of the countryside as I am, so sometimes I describe to them the flight of a bird, I can identify a birds by their flight, I will describe their nest and describe their eggs or the colour of the eggs to them. They may not be interested but I'm trying to make them aware of their surroundings.

Alan Lloyd, born 1936

I went to school in a town but I wasn't used to living in a town, so getting used to moving into a town was difficult. You had to be aware you had neighbours. I used to raise my voice and forget that there's somebody next door because when you were at home where we were, it didn't matter! You could have the stereo up as loud as you liked and no one would worry. That was something I noticed straight away. We lived in a small, three-bedroomed, semi-detached down in Headbrook in Kington and there was a house adjoining it and I can remember hearing things through the walls and thinking, 'Goodness!' I just wasn't aware of it at all. A small garden, hardly any garden at all … again everybody knows your business. The good thing about that is it's lovely to go up the street, everybody knows you, you're really part of the community and the spirit of the community. I love that. But there's a downside! Everybody knows everything. You can't do anything, and it took me an awful long time to get used to that.

Nicki Scott, born 1965

To finish, Nick Nenadich sums up the whole county vividly:

Until I went to the Bahamas I always thought that over the hill, and I don't mean into Worcestershire, there was something that was better, was more vibrant, more exciting, more 'me', you know. But having been to the Bahamas and all over the Caribbean and North America and all the rest of it, travelling around, South America, – [it was] amazingly interesting and they are all very beautiful and they've got their own unique beauty, they still don't … match Herefordshire. I thought Herefordshire was a one-horse town that I couldn't wait to get out of, but suddenly all the things about it seemed important and vibrant. When I came back I just remember looking at the fields and I just couldn't believe that rich depth of the greenery that you can only find in Herefordshire, and looking towards the Black mountains, going to play cricket and stopping at Capla. To look down the Wye Valley, going to Bromyard and standing on the downs, going to Kington up Hergest Ridge - everywhere you go in Herefordshire there is somewhere that is just fantastically beautiful and it was on my doorstep and it was always there and I couldn't see it. The simple things, like standing on the bridge at Lugg Flats and watching the water trickle over the gravel beds. It's just so alive to me now and just so breathtakingly beautiful and for me, those four years have put into context so many things that I was always running and hunting for, and I couldn't see them because they were just under my feet. It's a fantastic part of the world this. I don't say it's right for everybody but for me it doesn't get any better.

Nick Nenadich, born 1956

CHAPTER 2

House and home

Dennis Evans' home at Shobden.

Outside loos, and castles, modern and old. The people of Hereford discuss their homes:

Bulmers had a little estate of their own for their workforce and they were very good about that. But when Wiggins came, they moved into houses that Herefordians were on the waiting list for years – and the Wiggins people moved in and there was quite an uproar about that. Certainly there were letters to the paper . . . there was very bad feeling about that. You were on the housing list and then you came up on priorities. We had digs for the first year, then digs for another year until my first child was born, then we lived in a flat at the top of a three-storey house and in 1952 was the first time I got a house. We were waiting for five years and my husband, as an ex-prisoner of war, had priority and it still took us five years to get one.

Alvis Evans, born 1927

House prices have changed somewhat over the century:

The earliest house I remember was in Pengrove Road, Hereford. My father bought it in 1933 for £850, which he had paid for out of one year's profit. He was a saddler, a very skilled man. It was a three-bedroomed 1927 house and it had a very solid foundation. It was a very solid house and it had the sort of things like a copper to boil your washing in, in the kitchen, and it had a kitchen range which my mother used to stoke up and cook in. And it used to be a great pleasure to go into the kitchen when

you were small . . . sit in front of the kitchen range, it was so lovely and cosy and warm. The bathroom was like going into a deep freeze. There was no radiator. We had the gas geezer to provide the hot water. From time to time it used to blow up. The rooms were very, very nice. There was a nice entrance hall. It was a nice house. [We all] loved the house but father wanted something a bit bigger and when I was older he used to take me round to see these houses – 'This is the one we'll have John'. And we'd go to see the solicitor and we'd go and tell my mother and she'd refuse to move!

John Ellis, born 1931

Traveller Sam describes her wagon:

This is my home – it's based on a traditional barrel-top wagon. It's made with bowed wood with tarpaulin pulled and stretched over. I had the base made out of metal. There's motorbike wheels, there's wooden shafts for the horse to go into when she's pulling it. I made it so it's got lots of light. The tarpaulin over it is bright red. There's a bay window at the back which is above the bed, there's a little window for my daughter's [area] at the front because it's a three-quarter door, and another window. As you go inside you've got the burner and then there's ledges either side with my things on them. There's about a metre and a half between me and the bed and the door, and the bed pulls out so I can pull it out into a double bed if I want to. There's a bay window above the bed at the back of the wagon and underneath there's

Aerial view, Shobden, 1964.

another little arched window. I wanted to make the space as light as possible. I never get cold in here but in winter, life is spent wooding and feeding the horse. In the winter, the evening [is the best time] when all the work is done and the candles are on and it's glowingly warm in here and I can sit down and relax and I can do weaving, listen to tapes and learn tunes, and practise my pipes.

Sam, born 1967

We had a lovely house, a big house, cold as an iceberg! We didn't have electricity. My first memory are candles at night, which I always felt was a bit dangerous but we never bothered about it. We lit our oil lamps, it was part of life, a task to be done. We didn't have a bathroom as I remember. We all used to bath in a tin bath, and washing was a bit of a chore to say the least, but it had to be done on Mondays. Regardless of whatever happened, it had to be done on Mondays!

Gary Starkey, born 1951

The house where Andrew Morris was born, in Westfield Street, Hereford, had a sawmill and four big garages at the top of the garden. When he went into estate agency at the age of seventeen, he had a bright idea:

I said to my dad one day, 'Really dad, you should knock the sawmill down, knock the garages down and build a nice big house for us all!' And that's

25

what we did. When I was twenty-one, we designed mum and dad a nice house in the garden of our old house. [We] sold the old house to pay for the new house, and we lived there for another six years . . . I moved up the garden!

Andrew Morris, born 1950

I was born at Yew Tree Cottage, Kimbolton. It was just an ordinary cottage with a very large garden – a very good garden. Us boys used to have to plant enough potatoes to last the whole year round. It was close on half an acre. It used to take me a fortnight to dig it! It was a two-bedroomed house – we had a greenhouse there, I can remember, and

Cyril Bird at the age of four.

where we used to grind the corn and store the potatoes. There was a loft over the top and that's where we used to put the corn and then you put the corn into the mill down the bottom.

Cyril Bird, born 1921

We had a backyard, with a lavatory down the end, where you went in the middle of the night even when it was freezing cold. The only water supply was a tap in the middle of this yard and we used to seem to have more snows in those days than we do now because I can remember being nearly drowned in the snow trying to reach a frozen tap! The house was on three storeys. It was a dark house . . . you went in through the front door, down a deep passage. The parlour was on the right and then there was a curtain, and that was a horrible curtain to pass because the cellar was behind that curtain and as a child that wasn't nice – particularly on Fridays because that was bath and hairwash night and you got bathed down in the cellar. And to make sure you didn't catch cold, my mother used to sponge us down with a cold sponge! I can feel it now! It really was hateful. But a bath a week was pretty good - a lot of people didn't bath at all! Then into the kitchen-come-living room where there was the old-fashioned overmantel with the plush curtains with all the knobs on, the string where you dried your underwear, the scullery, and then out into the backyard and that horrible toilet at the far end. Upstairs I think there were two rooms on each floor . . . the top floor we weren't allowed to go up – which we did, of course. They used

Yew Tree Cottage.

to buy me dolls which I hated so my brother and I set fire to one and dropped it down the well of the house. We shared a room with my mother and father. My father worked away a lot so it was usually just my mother and we weren't allowed in my grandparents' bedroom. We stayed there till I was about seven, then we moved to Ross Road into a brand-new house where they'd got hot water baths. Wonderful! We moved in March 1935. It was a private estate. It had a big garden – at least I thought it was when I had to weed the damn thing! It was a three-bedroomed semi-detached. My father paid a massive sum of £540 for it.

Alvis Evans, born 1927

Kate Henning and her son, Caius Hawkins, live at Kinnersley Castle. Kate's father bought it after the war:

Big houses were so cheap after the war and all around us, big houses were being pulled down and I spent many years before we came here looking at extraordinary wonderful empty houses, magical places that had just been left empty since the war. I think this was the oldest one we saw. We saw it on a beautiful day, the sun was shining, the horse chestnuts were in flower and it even seduced my mother, which she lived to regret, but it really did look good that day. I guess it was everything he [my father] ever wanted really, but it was a wonderful old building and it offered the space. But I think he did have a sense of rescuing the building. People came up to me and say, 'Your father saved it'.

Kate Henning, born 1944

Kinnersley Castle is an unusual mixture of different ages of architecture. Also, it's a bit of a mystery, because we know it was rebuilt in the Elizabethan era by Roger Vaughn and it's got some very fine features from that era, but at the same time the stonework is a lot older, probably it's a couple of hundred years before then. But the shape of the building for example doesn't make sense in a lot of cases. It should have been a lot bigger. It's probably half the original size and also it's had bits added on later so it's quite an unusual building in the sense that you go round it and you're not going round a building from one particular era. You're going round somewhere that's part 1960s, part 1890s, part 1750s, and part mediaeval. I think it's great. I love it. If you are mad enough to keep a place like this going you're not going to worry what people think of it.

Caius Hawkins, born 1965

I was born at my grandmother's farm ... grandfather was a baker up in Presteigne and then he decided to buy this farm. Mother would have been about eight when she came to live here. It was a mixed farm, as most were in those days. I know we had sugar beet. I was very good at beet hoeing. I won competitions at 'Young Farmers' with hoeing beet. They were planted in a long line, much too close together, so you couldn't bend down and pick a few out. So you had this hoe which would be five, six inches wide and you used to pull it through the row and push it back again so you had a ridge and leaving (hopefully!) one plant, then a gap, then one plant again, and they would grow. Nowadays they have precision drills so they've cut all that out – but it was good fun. Our [Young Farmers] club were the first to do proficiency tests in basket making so we were quite proud of that. We had to do chores on the farm. We were three girls and my mother said she'd never have another one in case it was 'another bloomin' girl!' So, Saturday morning I should think I was the only girl from the grammar school out cleaning out the cow houses and sweeping the yard but, saying that, we used to argue about who was going out to help dad because if you were left inside you had to clean shoes and do all sorts of horrible jobs. I never drove a tractor, which I was disappointed about. My sisters did. I always fancied having a go at ploughing. I would have loved to do some ploughing. Perhaps I will one day. We had to get the sheep in and maggot them. That was a horrible job. It used to make me shiver. We never had a dog that was good with sheep. If you'd got a sheepdog, the dog does most of the work for you. But we didn't have a good sheepdog, so we girls had to be sheepdogs – and we were always running in the wrong direction or standing in the wrong place or something so it was quite a headache getting the sheep in. Then we penned them in the yard and I did a Young Farmers proficiency test in looking after sheep and I failed it because I didn't cut their toenails hard enough. I was there with the knife thinking, 'Poor sheep, I hope it's not hurting'. You'd have to throw one, and father would do that, and then we'd hold it while he was clipping, by hand, all the dirty potions and tails and things and sometimes, if he was wanting them to look extra specially good we had a hand-turned shearing thing and I'd be turning it and thinking about other things and getting slower and slower and he'd say, 'Faster!' and off we'd go again. We used to lug bales – we girls were able to load bales as good as any man. We were proud to boast about that.

Ann Jenkins, born 1939

I was determined that this should be [our children's] permanent home. Within three years, we had designed and built this particular property in Kington and I would be loath to leave it now. It was planned so that it could be extended, and although it looks like a bungalow, there is an upstairs to it. So it could be extended both outward and upward and it was planned accordingly. It took me about a fortnight to plan the shell of this because I had to look at other people's plans. I was amazed to find there were cavities in the walls, I had great difficulty in finding the ways the doors should open – something so trivial. And after about a fortnight I was so pleased with myself – the plan was all drawn – I went to bed, and suddenly woke up with a start. So much so I actually disturbed my wife, and I realised that after a fortnight I hadn't got an inside loo in this splendid new bungalow I was going to build because we had always had a 'ty bach' or an outside loo back at home! We only had

a certain amount of money. We purchased the land here for £250. We had to knock it down £15 because we couldn't afford £275. We used that as the deposit for the rest of the loan and it cost £2,122 for the land and the building. We built it ourselves and it took us eight months only. I was teaching at the time and it was mainly during the spring and summer months and I used to work till after midnight each day.

Alan Lloyd, born 1936

CHAPTER 3

Who are we?

Jill Southall and Ann Stokes' Herefordshire home, 1945.

Because of health reasons, my father was advised to move from Leicestershire and it was suggested he either moved to Wiltshire or Herefordshire. And he applied for a job in Herefordshire and got it – much to the surprise of many people in the area because usually when a farmer employed a bailiff he had either one of his own men or somebody from a neighbouring farm. So we were weirdos when we came!

Jill Southall, born 1938

Nobody in those days moved very far – you might move to the next village, the next estate but you seldom moved out of county. I wasn't excited because I knew I'd have to start again. We'd almost come to a different country.

Ann Stokes, born 1934

We had a different accent. I can't remember realising it was that different until my sister came home from school talking broad Herefordshire, 'I be, they be' this sort of thing, and my mother being absolutely horrified and my sister said, 'I'm fed up of being thought different' and my mother said, 'You can be different because you're not talking like that!'

Jill Southall, born 1938

I realised if I was going to survive at all at least I'd got to speak the language. Mother had brought us up to talk 'King's English' (it was then) but they were very dialectic here – 'How be thee? Where's

thee bin. She was sat'. It was the accent. You didn't go up a 'headland', you went up a 'hadland'. You went through 'glats' which was a hole in the hedge. There is no afternoon in Herefordshire – it's always morning or evening. I never really regarded it as home because I didn't really belong. I was the foreman's daughter, I was neither fish nor fowl. They'd got to suffer the foreman, but they weren't going to suffer his daughter.

Ann Stokes, born 1934

We're just walking past the garden front of Brampton Bryan Hall, which was built in about 1740 and hasn't really been changed architecturally since then. It's a fairly large facade with seven bays with a large pediment in the middle. We're now walking toward the ruins of the castle, the main feature of which are two round towers which were built in about 1310 by the first Harley who came to live here. This is where there would have been a portcullis, that ball-flower moulding (which is on Hereford Cathedral a lot) dates it to around the fourteenth century. The Harley name has been carried on this estate for nearly 700 years – which in itself is quite unusual. In 1307 it was the occasion of a marriage with the heiress to the Brampton family. Hence the village is called Brampton Bryan, and the Brampton family had been here since the Doomsday Book. What is quite unusual is actually having the same family having been here since [then] and as a result of that, the core of the estate has never been bought or sold – it's always remained in the same family. You'd feel pretty responsible if you were the one who let the link go for any reason

Brampton Bryan Hall and castle.

so I suppose it is a sense of responsibility but also a very nice responsibility to have. My father and I have tried to make the landscape change as little as possible and that I believe is one of the lucky things about having an estate. You can try and keep it looking beautiful, but admittedly it's my idea of what looks beautiful rather than anyone else's. The relationship my father had with the tenants (I would say) was outstandingly good. An enormous number of tenants on the estate came to his memorial service in the cathedral in Hereford. He was very good at getting on with people and it was very rare there was someone he couldn't get on with. The more old-fashioned tenants call me Mr Edward, some of them call me Sir, some call me Mr Harley and a lot call me Edward, and 'the Squire' sometimes. I really think it's up to people what they want to call me rather than what I want to be called. My father was called the Squire by a lot of people and inevitably

I've inherited that mantle with a few people. We do take tremendous trouble about the tenants we take on the estate. They are interviewed by the agent and they are separately interviewed by another member of the family which is usually my mother. We are trying to keep something a bit special going here, trying to keep a sense of community, and one of the ways you can do that is by getting people who have got children. We will always try to get a cottage, assuming it's a cottage away from the road, with a family with children. I would be very proud if I managed to keep this estate together for my successors. I would be very proud if I could achieve that.

Edward Harley, born 1960

The green baize door was as far as I went. You didn't go through the front of the house at all. You had the servants'

Doris Tunley marries in May 1956.

department, kitchen and scullery, and that was where you stayed … what was out of bounds was out of bounds … I had to work hard, my knees were sore. The kitchen floor had to be scrubbed out before breakfast, and it was a big room, stoke the fire up (it was an Esse cooker) and if the cook wanted to put on a boiled pudding and she thought there was a likelihood Mrs Pearson wouldn't want it she'd say to me, 'Hurry up, kid and get a saucepan of water and I'll tell her the pudding's already on!' If she said we didn't really want a suet pudding today she say, 'I'm sorry madam, we have to get it on early and it's already on'. She hadn't made it! That was a bluff! When Mrs Morgan come she wasn't 'Mrs' really but she put herself as 'Mrs' because it gave you more authority – we always called her Mrs Morgan – she was full of fun – and when we girls used to go out on our bikes, Mrs Morgan would put a fork or a spoon on the stairs – and if there was a fork, you went and looked in the Esse oven and there'd be a bit of something for you and if there was a spoon you went and looked in the servants' hall and you'd find a bit of something there.

Doris Tunley, born 1924

When we moved to Kinnersley, Herefordshire was extremely feudal and the expectations of how you lived in the big house were still so much in place. The estate had only been split up since the war so it had stayed the same since the Normans – you're talking about hundreds and hundreds of years of an attitude which is still there. Every now and then I do come across it and it knocks the breath out of me … there's still a lot of resentment. I started school very soon after we arrived here and went to the village school. That was unheard of, for anybody from the big house to go to the village school. The first morning, I remember, the teacher went out of the classroom and the whole class stood up and stared at me and then a little voice said, 'Are you a princess?' and I was totally unprepared for that. I didn't know how to handle it at all. I think it really made people feel quite insecure – the fact that Lord of the Manor and his family didn't behave in the way that they expected them to. That I didn't go to public school, that my father could be seen cycling to the post on a bike, and when we did have a car it was usually a pretty beaten-up old car. We obviously didn't have the money they always assumed went with a big house. I think my parents tried in the early years to maintain a bit of a pretence. We did the Christmas party for the school the first year, which was a bit embarrassing for me because I was actually at the school. My mother had to give every child a present – that was what was expected. The result was I didn't get a Christmas present that year because there wasn't enough money. It must have been really hard for my parents I think to find where they stood. It's so much easier now. I was a very lonely child. I didn't really have any close friends at school. I think parents felt embarrassed to invite me back to their houses because they were smaller. I picked up quite a lot of animosity from schoolteachers as well. It was like I wasn't supposed to be there, like I was a spy or something. I just wasn't playing the social game.

Kate Henning, born 1944

Some of us had the opportunity of taking the eleven-plus or entrance examination and I actually passed. I wasn't particularly happy about it because we were being taken out of our environment and the children in the town were very different. They spoke in a different way, they dressed in a different way. They were a little more 'slick' and worldly wise than we were – even in those days. So it was quite a cultural impact on me. I saw my first water toilet, for instance, at the grammar school at the age of eleven. The rural boys, for instance, had a difficult time at the grammar school at that period and it was mainly because of our background and the fact we were reticent. We weren't as vociferous as some of the others and therefore we were thought initially to have less ability. I did not have the opportunity to take external examinations in a grammar school, but a new head came in my fifth year and said 'you must all take external examinations and have an opportunity to better yourselves'. If that man hadn't come at the age of fifteen I would never have taken any external examinations.

Alf Jenkins

I remember at school they called me a gypsy – and that's one thing I'm not. I'm a showman's daughter. We are members of the Showman's' Guild of Great Britain. We have our own Padre, we have our own MP – we are just like any other party. I remember the indignation at school. I went home and I said, 'These children have called me a gypsy'. [My mother and my aunt] took me to school and we went to see the headmistress. She called all the children to the hall (there were about 150) and they explained in full detail my roots, my birth and my ancestry which goes back hundreds and hundreds of years from the first mediaeval jugglers in the street, the fire eaters, the ball rollers and the little hoop-la stalls and the roundabouts that were turned by hand. Yes, we can go back a long, long time. After that they said, 'Are you from a circus family?' I said, 'No,' but the Chipperfields and Billy Smart … they are … all related in one way and another … that's how showbusiness goes. There's no intermarriage. They are very staunch about that. They are religious … they don't go to church every week but they always insist on getting married in church, christened in church and buried from church. That is their three most important things. We have big gatherings of show people for funerals … it's respect. We have traditions, we're very staunch in our beliefs, we're a very close-knit family, very few divorces, very few marriage break-ups, and you always have to look after your own. 'Show people, fly-by-nights, Jack-the-lad, gypsies' – we've been called everything, even travellers – and we're not travellers because … they have nothing to do with show people. They fought in the wars, they died for their country, they have gone on to be MPs, barristers. We haven't all stayed in the show-land fraternity but it gave us a good grounding. I think we went to the university of life.

Jackie Danter, born 1944

CHAPTER 4

Money and the workplace

A business course in 1955.

Coracles, saddlery – and how not to use a Sten gun, cleaning out a de-feathering machine, and becoming a company director. The people of Herefordshire talk about the workplace and earning a living. John Ellis sets the scene in his family business, starting with a story from the First World War:

My father was in the trenches in the First World War … and he was due to go 'over the top' the next morning [again] and the Brigadier came down to cheer them up because morale was so low and he said to my father, 'What were you in Civvie Street, my boy?' And my father said, 'A saddler.' And he [the brigadier] said, 'What the hell are you doing here! We haven't got a saddler in the battalion!' So he pulled him out, he saved his life. Then after the war had finished he came back to Hereford and he went to work for a saddler in Broad Street – Mr James. Then Mr James died and Mrs James ran the business and after a little time she didn't want it anymore so my father bought it off her and then he went on for a bit. And then this colonel from Ross-on-Wye bought the whole block where our shop was, where I was born, and gave it to the dean and chapter so they could enhance the aspect of the west end of the cathedral – and eventually it was pulled down. Then my father had to find somewhere else and he didn't have any money, and he wanted to rent, but there wasn't anywhere to rent. But there was a shop for sale in Commercial Street which he eventually bought with borrowed money for £3,500. It's been there ever since and still is. My first memories [of the shop] was the smell of the leather – and the smell of the dye they used, it was quite different. There's no other smell quite like it. Those were my first memories. The other memories I have [are] of a man who worked for us for many years. I think he started when he was thirteen or fourteen and he finished when he was eighty. He was a master saddler as well. I remember seeing him with his white apron, stitching the harnesses they used to make. [In the shop] you'd have seen horse collars hanging up, a great big glass cabinet full of horse bridles and bits and head-collars. You would also have seen leather goods – handbags and travel bags, suitcases and sports goods – because it was allied to the leather trade. It was an interesting place.

People used to have a horse but not have the money to run it properly. It costs a lot of money to run a horse. I think some of them found it very difficult and it was more than they could afford. They used to buy the daughter a horse, or a pony, but as soon as she got a boyfriend she wasn't interested in the pony! There was enough business to keep it going – it was a good business, the saddlery business. People used to travel … they used to come for miles to a specialist shop. Leather came from a tannery in Devon, a tannery in Derby, and from Walsall. I knew of one tanner in Rhayder, a friend of my father's, and we used to buy some leather off him. I think it was sheepskins. The smell was awful! [Making a saddle] you start with the wooden tree and everything is built round the tree. The flaps were made of cowhide and the seat was made of pigskin. Then you made a pad and stuffed it with the lambswool. It was very skilled. We used to machine stitch, but I don't think you can machine stitch a saddle. We used to have a machine – the thread used to go through a bowl of hot black wax before it went into the needle so every stitch you put in was coated in wax. But that was for the heavy work. It was mostly sewn by hand. Certainly saddles were sewn by hand – because the stitching is on the inside, you can't see where the stitching is. Some saddles were imported from India. They were rubbishy ones really. My father used to sell a hunting saddle for £15 or £20 but now they are about £350 – it's incredible. There was an awful lot of work to make a saddle properly and I suppose a poor man's saddle he would probably buy second-hand anyway. He probably would never buy a new saddle.

John Ellis, born 1931

Peter has found a niche as one of the few traditional coracle makers left in Britain:

In 1987 I turned to coracle making. I really wanted to go down the River Teme (top to bottom, eighty miles) and from somewhere in my subconscious the idea of a coracle bubbled up and I eventually found a traditional maker at Ironbridge. I went to see him and saw one of his skin boats and that was it. That was what I wanted to build. I think it was the natural materials, the hazel, the willow, the cowhide. It was just an incredibly organic machine. Completely natural, nothing man-made in it. I thought, 'That's the boat. I'm going to make one of those and I'm

going to go down the river'. And I did. They are very ancient. The Romans write about them but I think they go back 10,000 years possibly. They are a very primitive form of craft to traverse large waterscapes. So I got involved, did the trip and then someone said, 'Will you make one for me?' And it went on like that and we eventually developed the business and we have a coracle society of which I'm chairman. I got involved in a big project last year. We built an eight-cowhide-skin boat which we sailed up from Scotland to Ireland. A prehistoric boat, basically. I'm probably the only person in the British Isles making skin boats in a serious way. It's become part of village life and a few other chaps in the village have got them and we go on the river together. I hold a coracle regatta every year in June and people come from all over the country for that.

Peter Faulkner, born 1942

Alvis Evans' war effort began with knitting socks and continued into the Home Guard which she joined as a teenager:

My father was in the Home Guard so, aged about sixteen, I joined. He'd just been made an officer. He was very patriotic. They decided to start a women's corp and my aunt joined and I wanted to join. Dad allowed me to make out I was eighteen, and my friend made out she was eighteen, and we joined. We trained as telegraphists and we had army drill so we knew how to march properly and we had weapons instructions and we used to go on the

Alvis Evans in the Home Guard.

assault courses with the RAF. There were about three of us under twenty and the rest were over fifty so you can guess who the lads helped! We had a great time. You were always very conscious that you did your bit for the war. I think I knitted that many pairs of woollen socks for the Navy it wasn't true – even at the age of twelve, I was knitting socks. Everyone wanted to do something for the war. You were very conscious of the war effort. We didn't get bombed in Hereford so we were lucky in that respect – but you did everything you possibly could. We used to do all-night

manoeuvres at the back of somebody's house in Bridge Street. You'd have radio telephones and you'd take the messages down and you'd relay them on to somebody else and there'd be several men on duty at the same time – elderly men – and my friend and I always managed to have this night duty and there'd be this little stove in the middle. We didn't take the messages – the men would take the messages and they'd make us cups of tea and tell us stories all night. We had a wonderful time! We had 300 rifles, not 303s – the Army had those and, in their wisdom, so we didn't get wet, we'd be underneath a corrugated tin roof, firing these rifles and the noise was terrific. On another occasion we used Sten guns and because bullets were short we were on automatic, not on repeat. We were all stood in a long line firing at biscuit tins. There was a line of women firing, and my friend's Sten gun, not being of the best quality, went from automatic to repeat- and she said, 'Oooh, it won't stop!' And I've never seen my father and the other men run so fast in their life. If she'd have come this way she'd have mown us all down. But it was good fun!

Alvis Evans, born 1927

Brian Cheeseley remembers how proud he was to be a telegram boy – and how he still enjoys delivering mail even now:

I've been a postman now for over forty years. The last seven [years] I've spent on Lugwardine and Mordiford delivery. I've certainly seen the changes. It was a wonderful job when I first started. Then we went through a very bad spell, changes and work pressures and things changed. Now we're slowly getting back to the way the job should be, which is a pleasure.

I was sixteen and was very fortunate I got a job as a telegram boy. It was after the war – everybody had the impression that telegram boys always brought bad news. We also took wedding telegrams, greetings telegrams, telegrams from the Queen. It was a wonderful feeling. You wore a crash helmet, gauntlets, leather jerkins and we had special little red bikes. There weren't many motorcycles

around in those days and we were the kings as far as we could see. I think it was the best two years of my life, in the Post Office. After that, the Post Office decided that they would teach me to drive (and the other lad that was on the motorcycles with me) and after we'd been taught to drive we'd become a rural postman straight away – we and the old boys, who'd been delivering these deliveries for years, and they took you under their wing. You'd become part of a group of four. You had a rotation of four jobs – two rural deliveries, one town delivery and one afternoon collection so you had a variety of work. There was no drink-driving laws in those days as such and there wasn't so much traffic about so you could have a drink on the way round. You'd stop at a pub and have your breakfast, but you daren't do that anymore.

Brian Cheeseley, born 1943

The Post Office was enjoyable then. It wasn't making a fortune but you enjoyed the job and it wasn't until the '70s when the job started to deteriorate. Jobs were getting heavier because it was increasing mail all the time. The Post Office wouldn't recognise the fact and unfortunately we did have our industrial relations problems. We've had our strikes and the major strike – I was on strike for seven weeks. The earlier '80s through to the early '90s, things were just getting more and more pressure on the postman to achieve more and more but the resources weren't put there to be able to achieve these things. Jobs were generally overloaded, especially in the town areas – they were terrific deliveries. They are getting better now and the job is beginning to become a pleasure again.

Brian Cheeseley, born 1943

On the whole you've got a sense of belonging – you belong to the Post Office, and especially after a long time, but you also belong to the people in the country. You're their postman. They look forward to seeing you every day. Very often you're the only person that goes to that house six days a week. If there is a problem they can ask you to help out or do something for them or fetch a bit of wood or carry something in for them. Once, many, many years ago I walked past a window and glanced in and saw a poor old lady lying flat on her back. Unfortunately she'd been there all night and nobody would have noticed her if I hadn't gone by at the time. I think it's part of being a postman, what a postman is all about. It's not just delivering letters. It's what you can give to the community at large. For me it's more of a vocation than a job. I had thought many years ago about going somewhere else but I'm glad I stayed and I'm too old to learn anything new now!

Brian Cheeseley, born 1943

Ed Clarke started on the shop floor at Sun Valley Poultry with the trials and tribulations of cleaning out the poultry de-feathering machine:

It was just inconceivable to live at home and not make a contribution to the home so I had to find a job quick and I came to Sun Valley because they had part-time night-cleaners' jobs going. As far as I was concerned it was something I was going to do temporarily while I was looking for something better. They gave me the job of cleaning out the de-feathering machines which was all muck and wet feathers – but they didn't give you any protective clothing such as hats so I used to go to where they bagged the chickens up and take one of the bags and put that over my head and whatever, because I had to crawl inside this machine and clean it out. These bags at the time were like 3p each because they were the turkey bags, so one of the daytime supervisors came to me and told me off about it, which I didn't receive too well. I was told to come in at 5.30 the next day and I'd have to go and see the production manager. I knew I was going to have this interview so I actually came in with my dark suit and stiff collar, looking very smart, thinking I was going to lose this job. Of course he recognised I was a bit out of the usual and I guess we were talking for about two, two-and-a-half hours. He finally said, 'Why don't you come and work for us permanently?' – and I said, 'I don't want to work in a factory'. He said, 'We're now starting to move beyond selling basic whole chickens. We've got this new customer, Marks & Spencer, and they want all sorts of hand-cut stuff and sooner or later we're going to have to develop it – so give it a go anyway!' That's what I did.

When I first joined Sun Valley, it was formed by a group of Hereford farmers, and all those farmers were military men: Colonel Corbett, Colonel Phillips, Captain Lowe, Captain Baxter – very regimented type of company. We used to have this dining room. It was like the secret room, you know? Everybody knew it was there but few had been privileged enough to see it or be part of it. If you became part of that group then you were really seen as part of the elite to the company. You'd arrive at ten-to-one, drinks first, gin and tonic – pink gin and tonic – here I was, lager and pint man, now I'm suddenly up here at lunchtime in awe of these guys. The colonels would be stood around talking business – and of course nobody was allowed to sit down till Colonel Corbett had gone to the table. You sat almost according to your rank down the table. It was privileged, but it was also a damn good communications system too. It wasn't done for the sake of people living it up at lunchtime. It was a time for people like myself and the factory managers to listen to what the chairman and the senior-rank people in the company wanted and what their views of things were. You had the opportunity over lunch to talk about new ideas and things – so there was a great deal of purpose to it although it was a sort of social event. Now it's e-mails, computers, mobile phones from anywhere in the world at any time. The opportunities for guys like myself in the early days was to move from one department to another in Hereford here – and that was as far as the excitement went – and your odd trip to London to meet the Marks & Spencer people, but today it's so much more than that. A really truly international company. Funny, I've had lots of opportunities to

go and live permanently in the United States but I don't know. My roots have been firmly planted here in Hereford. I ended up on the board of the company and I've been given a lot of privileges so I feel fairly proud of what I've achieved. There's something that definitely happens to you when you work for this organisation. It draws this commitment and loyalty out of you into it somehow. Deep down there's this great sense of loyalty still to the Herefordshire people and the people I've worked with on the factory floor in those early days.

Ed Clarke

Estate agent Andrew Morris always had an entrepreneurial spirit:

When I was twelve I decided to go and get a job and I asked the local milkman if I could work for him on a Saturday and Sunday. I stayed with him for ten years! I kept it going after I left school because it was good extra money. I was learning a lot more on the milk round than I felt I was at home – good manners to people, how to behave, dealing with money, giving people change. I also had a bit of luck when I was doing the milk round – at the age of thirteen, I thought, 'Well, I deliver the milk in the morning, I'm going to get a paper round at night'. In those days the *Hereford Evening News* was a massive paper. I remember at school, going to the printing part and I said, 'Print me some cards up' and I developed my own card, put it through lots of letter boxes and it said, 'If you want the *Evening News* delivered, see me. 'I remember when I started I had thirteen customers and when I sold it I had six quire (which is 150 papers) which I delivered every night except Sunday. That paper round belonged to me, not the *Hereford Evening News*, and I remember selling it when I was about eighteen, nineteen for £26, which was a lot of money. I was always keen to earn money in those days. It was a great feeling because then you could go and buy a record – 6s 8d was a lot of money in those days and you could buy the new Shadows LP or EP or whatever. I remember buying a guitar, a transistor radio so you could sit and listen to Radio Luxembourg under your pillow at night in the '60s. Remember the scooters, the Lambrettas, the Mods and Rockers? I remember buying my scooter from Geoff Bedford in Whitecross Road and I went to the headmaster and said, 'Can I drive my scooter to school?' and he said, 'Yes, but make sure you've got a crash helmet, make sure you don't give people lifts'.

Andrew Morris, born 1950

Andrew Morris, estate agent, in 1986.

He continues:

I left school not getting a GCE and I suppose when I got to an age where I had to decide, I had an uncle who was highly placed in the world of Sainsbury's. This is long before Sainsbury's came to Hereford, or came to Worcester. They were London, and I remember going on the train to London for an interview at Sainsbury's in Blackfriars, and I was offered a job as a trainee manager and I came back on the train and I thought, 'Crikey, I've got this job! What do I do? I've got to give up my paper round. I've got to give up

my milk round. I've got to not do any more football'. Coming back on the train I thought, 'I'm not going to take it. I'm going to stay.' That night I read the *Evening News* and it said, 'Clerical Assistant Required at Russell, Baldwin & Bright' and I wrote this letter in my back garden and posted it, was invited down for an interview and was fortunate enough to get the break. I think I got the job because I'd worked under my own name since I was thirteen. You needed, in those days, not so much academic qualifications but you needed a bit of drive, determination, enthusiasm, commitment, personality, and I think that's what they saw and that's what I tried to give.

Andrew Morris, born 1950

Bulmers was the biggest employer in Hereford at that time:

A greater majority of the people worked at Bulmers and it was natural to go there… I started there in 1951 and I went to work in the laboratories, then out into the factory. I went into what they called 'processing' and progressed on from there. I'm the cider maker now. Bulmers fashioned most people's lifestyle and almost controlled their living standard, because they were the biggest employer here. What they paid was the going rate for the town so I think they had a great influence on the city. They've always been a good company to work for, a compassionate company. Of course, in the days when I first started there it was long hours work, compared to today. People travelled quite a long way to come in to work for Bulmers – twenty, thirty miles away. Much of the work was labour intensive, like the bottling lines, they used to be all young girls from school used to go there, and they had a reputation – 'Bulmers Angels' they were called! When I first went there, all the manufacturing was done at Ryeland's Street. There were two cider mills [there] … the apple storage, the vat house and all the cider was processed and packaged at Ryeland Street. The process was that different. We used to produce Pomagne and that used to be done by the Champagne method… my first job there was going round the cider mills sampling the pomace and taking samples back to the laboratory. It was basic in those days.

Cedric Olive, born 1935

We take the apples, we wash it and we mill it into a pulp – and that's where the process changes. In the old days it used to go onto the old rack presses where men used to build the cheeses up, fold the mash inside cloths, put wooden racks on them and the press used to go up and squeeze them one at a time – very manual, very physical. Now we just mill the pulp on a continuous moving belt and it presses continuously. That makes it that much easier. Where we used to have fourteen presses in the mill to do about forty tons an hour, we do sixty-three tons an hour these days with four presses in the mill … back in 1968 when I had a day and a night shift running, I'd have 170 men in there. Now, on a day and night shift I've got about twenty-four – that's the difference.

Cedric Olive, born 1935

I do worry what's going to happen to the society we live in now, because I don't see anybody entrepreneurial, professional in the ages of twenty to thirty in this town that are going to be here to take it on when I've died. I said to my son at Christmas, 'Do you want to come and work at Dad's estate agency? In twenty-five years time I want to retire!' And he said, 'Oh no Dad – it's hard work, you're never off the phone, you're never here'. They haven't got that dedication, that total commitment. The age group of fifteen to twenty-five now are totally different from when I was fifteen. We were all intent on getting business, getting jobs, leaving school and finding an opportunity within work. I think far more children

Cedric Olive, National Service, 1954.

nowadays go onto higher education, they go onto university, they'll come out of that at twenty-three, twenty-four years of age and haven't got a clue what they are going to do. It irritates me. I think, 'Crikey – when I was twenty-three, twenty-four, I was earning a lot of money because I'd got a good job, and these guys are going to be twenty-three, twenty-four and not know what they are going to do.' In the trade now I would say I don't like people if they are not disciplined. I like to see somebody well groomed, well clothed and I like to see somebody knowing what they can do and doing it correctly. There are people who like to play with jobs these days and estate agency has been one of those where people have tried to climb onto the bandwagon, haven't been properly trained and they try to get away with getting rich quickly and it hasn't worked, particularly in the late '80s with the boom and you saw all these firms springing up, particularly in Hereford, and those firms are no longer with us. They didn't know how to do the job properly and they were found out. This job of estate agency is a marathon and not a sprint, and you've got to go the distance to gain your reputation, to gain goodwill, and that's something I've always tried to do – and I've been doing it for thirty years and I'm always trying to portray the right image, the right commitment to people.

Andrew Morris, born 1950

All I ever wanted to do was be a pharmacist. It was really strange. I had this set idea I was going to get my degree, work as a pharmacist, earn loads of money, have this great career – and it hasn't worked out like that! I worked full-time as a pharmacist for four months in Merthyr Tydfil and it was a good job. It was a great place to work. The staff were brilliant and they taught me an awful lot about how to do the job but it was very stressful. It wasn't particularly long hours, I was only doing thirty-seven-and-a-half hours a week, but I was exhausted. I was so tired and I was getting really down and fed up and I think if I had stayed I would have ended up with depression. I thought, 'No, it's a well-paid job but it's not worth the money if I'm going to be ill at the end of it'. My mum was really quite scared. I was giving up a well-paid job – and when I decided to quit Merthyr, I didn't have another job to go to. I was giving up £20,000 a year – and straight out of college – that's not bad. I was prepared to give that up without having a job to go to and not knowing what I was going to do. It was a big step because I'd always wanted to make money and have a really good career but it's not worth getting ill over. I had never been depressed and if the cost of earning £20,000 a year is you have to take tranquillisers, every day it's not worth it. As a pharmacist I was selling a lot of herbal remedies, Bach Flower Remedies, homeopathy, which I knew nothing about because they don't train you about this stuff, apart from 'It's not to be touched, it's not to be trusted'. I knew nothing so I had to find out. There was an aromatherapist working not too far away, so I went and booked an appointment and I was so impressed because within a matter of about two months I was calmer, more able to cope with the job. I'd always had headaches –

they went. It was just brilliant! I thought, 'Wow, this stuff really works. I want to do this'. It was a big step because there's this feeling with some people it's 'medicine woman' stuff and not really acceptable but no one has given me a hard time. You train as an aromatherapist at college and wherever you go and you look at the prospectus there's always been this bit where they tell you how you are supposed to set up your company and how to run your business and they always forget to tell you this on the course. So I made it up as I went along. I had a bit of help because my parents set their own company up so I used their printer and their accountant. When I wanted equipment or stationary, my parents had loads of catalogues – so I've been fairly lucky – but it's how to advertise and how to market yourself. I haven't seen that much help available. I try to do it on my own and that has been hard. I did decide, and that was a conscious decision, that I would not market myself as the cheapest aromatherapist in the area because I don't want people to come to me because I'm cheap. I want people to come to me because I'm good. Now, if that takes longer to build up, fair enough. That is the way I want to do it.

Helen Winterbottom-Pope, born 1972

I biked to Tenbury School and that meant I could get a job as an errand boy in the evening. I used to work at a local grocery shop called Gaius Smiths, which were a big store. I'd start at four o'clock and finish at half-past five every night, apart from Thursdays, which was a half day. And all day Saturday for 10s. It was a good way of earning money – for half a crown or the 10s you could have all the entertainment you wanted. It was only sixpence for the pictures. A fair proportion went on clothes because you'd have to buy clothes yourself anyway. They had a bakery attached and they wanted somebody in the bakery and it wasn't as though I'd planned out to be a baker. The job was there and it was available and the money seemed reasonable at the time. I finished on the Thursday and started work in the bakery on Friday. I started at eight o'clock because under the Women's and Young Person's Act in those days you couldn't start before eight o'clock till you were sixteen and then you could start at six o'clock. There was only one baker in there. He was quite old – he'd been through the 1914-18 war as a fifteen-year-old and Harry Bayliss must have been seventy-plus. We got on well. He never spoke! He just occasionally grunted! He was a kind man and I think he tolerated me.

Jim Franklin, born 1940

The golden figure in the late '50s was £1,000 a year. This was almost unbelievable if people earned £1,000 a year – it was an horrendous amount of money. That was about the only time that I got enthusiastic about money. People would say, 'Did you know so-and-so is earning £20 a week!' 'No, he can't earn that much!' You used to think, 'What are you going to do with all that money?' It was an almost impossible sum to think about. By 1959, I'd learnt most of what I could. Another apprentice had started in the bakery so I wasn't really needed then. You were always levered out because now your wages were a lot more money and they could get an apprentice a lot cheaper. You weren't asked to leave but it was made quite difficult [to stay]. Then I got a job at De Greys in Ludlow as a 'journeyman'. 'Journeyman' came from the very old apprentice scheme where you learnt your apprenticeship, then you went on a tour round several bakeries to learn different skills. I started there Easter, 1959. By 1961, I'd got up to £1,000 a year and this was a great achievement! This was only done by working eighty hours a week, probably eighteen hours a day. On a Friday we would start at five o'clock in the morning – we would work right through till Saturday morning at ten o'clock. It's very strange because just at this period of time people are under so much pressure at work which is really completely unnecessary. Their working life is much more stressful, be it self inflicted, or inflicted from their bosses, so I find that the times now are no different from working a hundred hours. If you are working forty hours and under stress, it's probably equivalent to working a hundred hours and not under stress physically. I don't think there's a lot of difference really.

Jim Franklin, born 1940

A *final word from Jim:*

The biggest influence possibly I had for starting a bakery up was a visit to France in the early '60s. This was quite an eye opener. Every village had a little tiny bakery and it was a very basic bakery but they supplied the bread for the local village and I think that's where I was inspired, really, and thought that it could be done. Youth had never had the opportunities it had in the '60s. It appeared that the youth, whatever it did, just couldn't go wrong. So we went along with this. Sometimes in the quiet of the night you'd think, 'Good God, I'm a businessman!' You were juggling money, you were getting bank loans, so you didn't really have time to sit down – and every new member of staff you got, you thought you'd have more time. You didn't, you had less time. You don't realise, you're on a very big learning curve when you are going into business at that rate, and you are keeping everybody afloat and you're also dealing with quite a large volume of money, plus you're dealing with legislation – with so many aspects of business. Providing you don't lose sight of the fact: 'Who you are, what you are'. There are probably stages where you get bigger than your boots but as long as it doesn't last too long and you're brought back down to exactly what you are, I don't think you've got any problems.

Jim Franklin, born 1940

CHAPTER 5

Living together

The wedding of Alvis Evans' parents, 1924.

Getting married, getting divorced, having babies, life, loves, tragedy and death. Herefordians share their thoughts on living together:

I was one of the first, actually. In fact most of my friends still aren't married and have no intention or designs of doing so. I mean, my mum married when she was nineteen, which I think is stupidly young. Gosh, nineteen! I think if I'd got married at nineteen, I mean – wow – it doesn't bear thinking about. We met in the second year of university, and towards the end of the year you start working out where you are going to live in the third year and I couldn't find anywhere and I said to Jason, 'Why don't we get a place together?' I remember the look on Jason's face – as if he'd just been told he was Jesus or something. It was complete shock. Then [he] decided this might be a good idea, it could be good fun. We had a mediaeval wedding at Caerphilly Castle, just outside Cardiff. I never wanted to get married in church. Not being a Christian, getting married in church would have meant nothing to me. I always fancied the idea of getting married in a castle and this was before the law changed. Now you can get legally married there but that didn't change until a few months after we got married … so we had to go to the registry office in the morning and we had three friends with us to sign the register and that was it. Then in the afternoon we all got dressed up and I went and got my hair done and my make-up done and then we had a mediaeval wedding at the castle and for that we actually wrote the vows ourselves and we had a friend of ours

officiating and it was really stunning. I kept my name and then I added my husband's name on, so it's now hyphenated – Winterbotham, which is me, and Pope, which is his family. Someone said recently … they thought this was wrong and they thought we should take our husband's name but I don't see why you should because I don't suddenly stop becoming Helen Winterbotham and become Helen Pope. I'm still the same person and at the end of the day I am a Winterbotham. There's definite traits that come with the name Winterbotham and I've got all of them – good, bad and indifferent! And I just didn't want to give that up.

Helen Winterbotham-Pope, born 1972

Sam is a traveller. She discovered a partner with a like mind:

We used to do a lot of busking – that's where I learnt music, and we were really discovering things. We'd talk a lot about the earth and the sacred places, the stone circles and the earthworks and the ancient cultures and all that sort of understanding, and seeing the world and the earth and its spirits in a completely different way – in a way which our ancestors used to, and not underrating their intelligence.

Sam, born 1967

I was 'released' from home and found my feet and made this step into marriage quickly, possibly too quickly, who knows? She was seventeen and I was twenty-one, something like that, and not having been away from home before, it was a major step. I would suggest to you it benefited us because we had to stand on our own two feet. We were naturally aware of our financial restraints. Mother was very possessive, and rightly so, but I didn't appreciate that at that time … Angela, my wife, was only the second girl I'd ever known and taken out – ever known – only to hold hands and possibly to kiss – incredible looking back in those days. We were not experienced in any way from a physical or sexual point of view and we went into marriage with no ideas. [My first girlfriend was] the daughter of a friend of my mother's and it was thought that she was too young. Almost on the rebound I went towards Angela, mainly because one of my friends said, 'There's an Italian family, just arrived. I wonder who's going to be first to take out the girl there!' Of course, that was a challenge and we were married six months later. As a Welsh-speaking person, I could communicate in English fairly well but here was a person who could speak hardly any English, but Italian … we had to work hard at our marriage and that's possibly why it has survived forty years.

Alan Lloyd, born 1936

Family expectations about being in the family way:

I put on a lot of weight about twelve months ago and over the space of two weeks I'd spoken to three different friends … and I said, 'I've put on loads of weight' and the next question was

'Are you pregnant then?' And [I said] 'No, I'm just getting fat. Why does that mean I'm pregnant?' I don't see why that should be the first thought in anyone's mind and my mum and my grandma have been asked on a few occasions whether I'm pregnant yet because, hell, I've been married a whole three years! Surely I should be breeding by now! And it really annoys me. It's nobody's business but me and my husband's. There is this social idea that if you are married, a family follows and you couldn't possible be married for any other reason than to have kids and actually I married because I want to spend the rest of my life with this person – not because I want to have children. If I'd wanted children I could have had children without getting married. I mean … my grandma, maybe she's just a bit different, but her attitude is I should avoid having children as long as humanly possible. I think because I have the choice not to – she didn't have access to contraceptives … you didn't do that sort of thing – and I have the choice. I don't have to have a child if I don't want to. I think there is perhaps an element of [that] it would have been nice for her to have had that choice.

Helen Winterbotham-Pope, born 1972

Anne Stokes wanted children but the odds were not in her favour:

We were snowed in and I didn't really realise I was pregnant until, it was about February, and we still couldn't get out and I said to my husband, 'Oh, leave it'. And when I did finally get to the doctors he reckoned I

Ann Stokes with her sister, Jill, and parents, 1944.

was about four-and-a-half months pregnant. I have very bad blood pressure, which didn't help. Also, I haven't got very good stomach muscles so there was far too much room for him – and he wasn't a very big baby and he had plenty of room to move around. He got the cord very tightly round his neck in the end. Of course there were no scans to tell us that. Because we had this house and we had hot water and a flush toilet (we hadn't got electric light in those days) it was decided I would be suitable for a home confinement, which I did have. It was nobody's fault that he'd got the cord so tightly round his neck. It was round ten times in the end and of course he was starved of oxygen so he was a spastic. They took him into hospital, but again, incubators were quite crude and there was very little they could do. But there was a lot of

good came out of that because, with another woman and the help of the paediatrician we started the Spastics Society in Herefordshire. It's still going – and we raised enough money to build a holiday home in Towyn which is still going – and he died when he was four … when he was about two, I was pregnant again. That was dreadful. I had very severe blood pressure. I went into hospital and I knew the midwives and I said to them, 'There's something wrong here'. They agreed with me. I asked for an X-ray, but they didn't like X-rays in those days. Anyway, they did it. Part of the back of its head was missing. The brain hadn't developed. The obstetrician said, 'What are we going to do?' I said, 'I don't want a Caesarean – that's going to be ridiculous. Let's see what happens'. So I sat there for a fortnight and nothing happened. Well, it doesn't you see. The hormones aren't right. So I had to have what's called an induction, and I hold the record (so I'm told, still). I had six inductions and none of them worked. That's castor oil, very hot baths and an enema – I had four of those and they … broke my waters and it still didn't work. So then they tried a very revolutionary procedure called an epiticine drip. It was very crude at the time but it worked. I had to have the houseman – he had to sit beside me the whole of the time this drip was in and I had to have it all the way through the labour. It was very, very painful, but it worked. The child lived – but he couldn't survive for very long outside me. I think he lived for about half an hour. They did nothing, and the midwife (I knew her) said, 'My God girl, if you're doing the job you do do it well don't you!' I said, 'Thank you'. She said, 'This is not going to live very long' … I desperately wanted children. That was the whole idea of getting married. My husband had talked to the obstetrician and he had said 'no more' … [so] we adopted two and I'm very proud of them, very proud. Our son was asked what he thought about being adopted and he said, 'Life's a lottery and I've won first prize!'

Ann Stokes, born 1934

Ann and Jill Stokes in 1941.

Alvis Evans' wedding, 1948.

Someone said 'Why don't we go busking in Oxford?' and that week my boyfriend came home and discovered I'd gone away and he freaked out and trashed everything I owned. Everything. I was giving up smoking in that week too. I didn't start again but it was interesting because at first I was furious but then later that night we were just cheering – we were going, 'Yes! Freedom!' I had what I had – sleeping bag, backpack, instrument, money we were making busking.

Sam, born 1967

Alvis Evans had a frightening experience with her husband:

My husband was in a prisoner-of-war camp for most of the war. He was captured in January 1940 and he was released at the end of April 1945. I didn't know him till later and I think it would be in 1954, '55, he had three or four months' absolute hell because he started having terrible nightmares. He was a mild-mannered man … I woke up twice [and] he'd [try to] throttle me. If I'd not been stronger he would have killed me. He would have been hanged for that because I never thought to go to a doctor and say what was happening to him. He used to have these tremendous nightmares – I was a German – I could hear it said – and I used to get out of bed, tie the children's bedroom door to the bathroom door so there was no way he could get at them, then wake him up, run outside the bedroom and just hold the door tight, so he couldn't get out till he woke up properly. It took ten or fifteen minutes and he went like that every night for four or five months. It was horrible to see him in those nightmares. I couldn't have left him sleep and not wake him up out of them because it was too bad. Whether I'd have been better off doing that I don't know. But, as I say, twice he strangled me. You didn't think of getting help from anyone. You just didn't. I told my mother-in-law years after and she said, 'Oh, I should have warned you. The doctor told me it would happen'. My family never knew – it was disloyal. You didn't do that. Nobody knew. I had to work at my marriage. Everybody's marriage goes through a bad time and I think if more people stuck to that now it would be better. I think it's too easy – but – at the same time, my husband's situation, emotional help would have done wonders for him. He needed it. It wasn't there. I never thought to go to a doctor. You just didn't … I was talking to a girl on the bus who was going to buy a wedding dress, and then they were going to the estate agents to buy the house. She said, 'I want to make sure it's in my name as well as my husband's' and I said, 'Why?' and she said, 'When we get divorced … ' Not 'if' – 'when'. Now divorce was a filthy word in our day. If you got divorced you'd failed your marriage, you'd failed to cope with life as it was. You did not give in. You just did it.

Alvis Evans, born 1927

I'm still the person I was before I got married, I'm still me. And I don't see why people should alter the way they treat you, just because you've got married. But my friends round here they won't ask me out … to go anywhere really. They'll go out to nightclubs and they won't think of [asking me]. It's like, 'I'm married therefore I wouldn't want to go to a nightclub' – because I don't need to pick anyone up, or something, I don't know. I don't really see why it should make a difference. I can leave my husband at home – I'm not chained to him. We're not a single entity. We do a lot of stuff together because we have the same interests but we also are separate people as well and I really think we should be treated as separate people.

Helen Winterbotham-Pope, born 1972

Alvis Evans with her family in the 1970s.

A family get-together for Ann Stokes in 1967.

To finish, the story of a slight misunderstanding:

At the mother and baby home we did have people in who really didn't know [about giving birth] … I used to have to talk to all the girls. I did the sewing, the mending while I was there and they'd come and talk to me. I was talking away to [one of the girls] one day and I said, 'You know that in about a month's time the baby will be born?' and she said 'Yes' and I said, 'You're not very sure of your dates are you?' and she said 'No' and I said, 'Well, it'll be about a month we think. Do you know what will happen?' 'Well,' she said, 'You have to put a zip in first don't you?' and I said, 'No, no zip' and she said, 'How does it come out then?' and I said, 'Same way as it went in!' I'll never forget her face! She sat down in the chair and said, 'But it can't! It's only a little hole!' and I said, 'It'll get bigger. Don't worry!'

Ann Stokes, born 1934

CHAPTER 6

Crime and law

Hereford policewomen in the1940s.

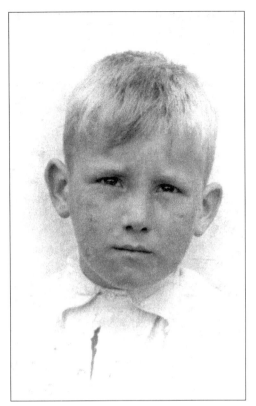

Cedric Olive, at the age of six, in 1941.

From problems of being the local policeman's daughter and scrumping apples, to the role of women in the police force. The people of Herefordshire discuss their misdemeanours:

As lads we scrumped apples. I can remember going to one farmer and pinching the apples in his orchard. These apples used to rot on the floor and I used to pinch them. I was surprised when he kicked me up the backside. I must have been thirteen or fourteen and I said, 'Look at all those apples, wasting'. And he said, 'I'm kicking you up the backside because you are breaking my hedges. Go through the gate and that will be okay'. And when I went the next time he again kicked me up the backside and I asked

him why and he said, 'You can take apples, but not by the sackful!'

Alan Lloyd, born 1936

Has respect for the police altered so much over the century?

Respect for the police was different in those days. Inspector Bob James used to live over the Moorfield side there, Wally Burton used to live up Cotteril Street, and we only had to see them and we would run, no matter what we were doing. They were policemen and we were kids and we'd run. Bob James always had two spaniel dogs and if we were over at the dam on the brook where we used to play for hours we'd be fishing, and we'd see his dog come up there – we'd scramble and hide. We weren't doing anything wrong but we'd run – we'd have that respect. If you see Wally Burton coming up on his bike, he'd never done anything to us, he'd caught us a few times and told us off and clipped us round the ear. It was just that respect you had. There was nothing wrong with that, nothing wrong.

Cedric Olive, born 1935

Lynne Hunter had a slight dilemma:

I always knew when things had gone too far – if my friends were throwing stones or knocking on little old ladies' doors, I knew that was wrong and I knew I would get into more trouble than anybody else, being who I was, so I had to shut my eyes and not always tell. There were incidents when my father had arrested my friend's father. Obviously because it was a small community I was a little on the outside looking in. That was quite hard. I don't think I ever had a best friend. Dad used to like me to have nice friends but he just knew everybody. He was a beat policeman, so he was often around. Walking home from school I would often see my father, which was another reason why I could never get up to no good! He was very much a community policeman. In the shops, chatting, he'd see a drunk on the side of the road, sort him out, tell him to go home and that sort of thing. It tended to be drink-orientated crimes. In those days as a policeman, especially in a place like Ross-on-Wye, you almost became friends with your criminals. I mean, not if it was bad, but petty theft and things like that you'd say, 'Hey, mate, don't do this again' – and the way police were allowed to discipline in those days – they were probably a little bit afraid of him, a little bit in awe, but also respected him.

Lynne Hunter, born 1959

It's been a privilege to have a policeman on the street that you recognise. You know that they'll be there, they know you, they know the family and they can keep down crime by just being there because the children realise they know them and the family. But because of the trend into more centralised policing in a small market town like Kington, the police and the police station is constantly under threat. I feel that crime will escalate as a direct result of having individual policemen here who don't know the area and the people in the area and haven't been here for years and

years. I would suggest that some of the elderly in our community (although this is a relatively quiet area) are a bit concerned about going out at night. I wouldn't have considered that even ten years ago.

Alan Lloyd, born 1936

Being a policeman's daughter stood Lynne in good stead when she encountered a 'flasher':

I felt very safe where we lived in Ross. I always did, and as a result I used to walk to and from school and it was quite a long way. It was a fairly busy road, but I never felt frightened, and one day I was walking down and a man went into a telephone box, which was probably

Lynne Hunter at the age of six.

NEW INSPECTOR RETURNS TO STREET OF MEMORIES

Son follows father in police service

BY BILL TANNER

A LIKE-father-like son link to policing Herefordshire sees newly appointed Inspector Howard Owen returning to where it all began.

Insp. Owen is now based at Hereford's central police station complex — built on the site of the old Delacy Street police houses that form some of his earliest memories.

The street has now vanished from city maps, but in the mid-1950s it was where a very young Insp. Owen, originally from north Wales, lived while his father Eric pounded local beats as a PC with the old Herefordshire Constabulary.

"My father was a widely respected man and I suppose, because of that, there was never much doubt that I would join the police as well," he says.

Taking memories of life next to Hereford's former Gaol Street police station, now the Magistrates Court building, the Owen family eventually left the city in 1963 and moved to another police house in Ross-on-Wye, where PC Owen senior was to work for 14 years.

After education at Ross Grammer School, Howard Owen joined the Merchant Navy for three years of seeing the world before following in his father's footsteps.

Since 1973, his life with the police service in West Mercia has taken in work with specialist traffic and motorway teams, and a two year detachment with the helicopter air support unit as an observer.

The father of three, and holder of an ecology degree, comes to Hereford after promotion through the ranks with time spent in Droitwich, Bromsgrove, Worcester, Redditch and Kidderminster.

"I'm very pleased to be back here after so long. Of all the postings I wanted on promotion, Hereford was my first choice," he said.

Insp. Howard Owen (right) the ne inspector with Hereford Police, and h father Eric, ex-Hereford and Ross PC.

The city's old Delacy Street police houses. Picture courtesy the "Hereford Then and Now" series by Derek Foxton.

A newspaper cutting, from 1993, about Lynne Hunter's father.

halfway down this hill, and I looked at him and I remember thinking, 'Why isn't he facing the phone?' He was facing outwards and as I approached him he was flashing at me and I can remember my dad always saying – because he used to joke about things – 'Do you know, when women get flashed at they can never remember the guy's face!' So I stood there for what seemed like a lifetime but it was only seconds and I looked this guy

in the eyes – I was petrified and then I ran, and I ran and ran, and I got to my mum's and I was so shocked. I suppose I was fairly sheltered – so shocked at what this man had done. Eventually she rushed me over to the police station. They popped me in a police car to see if he was still there and they found 'evidence' in the phone box and that made Dave, the policeman, very cross. So he took me to some people's houses and he said, 'Now, when they answer the door, I want you to tell me if it's the man'. So, of course I got to see people I didn't know were flashers as flashers! Anyway, it wasn't him. Then I had to give a statement to a lady policeman, which I found quite hard to do. I remember her asking me, 'What would you like to call it my dear?' and I said 'I'll call it a penis'. 'Okay' she said, 'Because obviously we'll have to refer to it several times'. They did catch him and my dad was thrilled. It seemed like a huge drama at the time and I think it's something these days we would deal with in perhaps a lesser way but it was a huge, awful thing to have happened and I was really, really frightened and I can remember this protective shell being put over me, by my parents, by the other policemen, the school as well, too. I think the impact it would have on a child now would be the same as it had on me. It's a shame crimes like that aren't treated as seriously as they were then. The reason is because there are such heinous crimes going on in the world now, we think of flashing and petty theft as not so important, but they are and they do have a devastating effect.

Lynne Hunter, born 1959

When I was about eleven, a couple of old houses were knocked into one. My father had then become the police sergeant in charge there. We went from a fairly comfortable house to one which was much bigger but far less comfortable. It had a cell. The cell was where we detained suspects overnight before they went to be tried at court, or

Joan Thomas and family. Joan's mother was the police matron.

Joan Thomas' father, who was in the police force in the 1900s.

An 'arresting' shot of Beryl Baxter, the actress, in 1947.

dealt with in any way. My mother was called the Police Matron. It meant that if we had any women detainees, she was allowed to search them – men were not allowed. The cell was very dark and dismal and it had iron bars and the only consent to furnishing was a wooden bed and a wooden pillow. What I do remember is my mother taking into the detainees a tray on which she'd put a silver teapot, tongs and cube sugar, tea and coffee and biscuits. I used to say to my mother, 'I think you'd let them sleep in one of our spare rooms if you could!' The irony of that was, she'd take this through and then say to us, 'I suppose you want a drink, too'. She'd say, 'Go into the pantry and get the mug out and don't spill it on the oil cloth!'

Joan Thomas, born 1925

Policewomen had a different role to play then. They didn't go on the streets. They were there as the soft side of the police force. I remember this 'auntie' of a policewoman coming to interview me and I felt very comfortable with her. She was lovely. And then there were the policemen who were the stronger image. It's not about equality. It's just about role-play, and women are significantly better at certain things than men and men are naturally better at certain things than women, in terms

Policeman Dennis Evans on duty in 1957, when the Queen and Prince Phillip came to Hereford.

of strength and power – physical power. So I think there are defined roles to be had. Not in all professions, but certainly I think in the police world there is a need for a soft side to the police force when women know that they can go to a policewoman who will be gentle with them and hasn't been out on the street and got loads of street cred but somebody who they know they can just fall into their arms and cry to and I don't think that's there so much now.

Lynne Hunter, born 1959

Kay Williams became the second female police officer in Herefordshire in 1946. However, her expected role was not quite what she had in mind:

If I tell you that when I went to be measured for my uniform it took an inspector and a sergeant four times to take my measurements – you can perhaps understand from that what they really thought. The older men that had not been in the war, they just laughed at us basically and thought we were a bit of sport as well. The policemen coming back into the force from the forces, they seemed to think we were comfort for the troops too. They'd had them in the services, hadn't they, during the war, and when they were demobbed (which was just at that time – '46). I think they thought, 'Great, we've got a bonus here, we've brought the WAFS back home with us!' We did all the things the men did – general beat duty, occasional point duty if there wasn't a policeman available. We did a stint on the switchboard of course, in the office, and generally on cases – being called to rape cases and the various sort of cases that happen today. One of the things that I hated was going on market duty. I hated that because I hated to see the cruelty there was there and I hated the Welsh farmers who thought we were there for a bit of sport and would actually run their hands over us! That wasn't pleasant.

Kay Williams, born 1924

And the technology was not always there to support:

You were asked to do decoy work. I have walked round and round the Castle Green when they were hoping to catch men that have attacked females. I've had to go dressed up to the nines, and plenty of makeup on, and saunter round and round and hope that I was attacked, and I found that a bit unnerving, I must confess! You couldn't even look over your shoulder because you were not supposed to do that sort of thing. But I did know that up some of the trees there were CID men, waiting to pounce. And I had got a whistle that I could blow but of course we didn't have handcuffs. I don't know how we were supposed to get people back to the cells with no handcuffs! Isn't that extraordinary when you think about it!

Kay Williams, born 1924

Violent crimes may be on the increase in this century:

When I started working in newspapers, a rape case was a rarity. I worked in Loughborough for a while. I don't remember a rape case during the nine months I worked in Loughborough. But rape now is very commonplace. You can pick up even your local paper, even the Hereford Times, and most weeks [it] has got a rape story or an attempted rape story. Those cases were so rare when I was a young journalist in mid-Wales. I just don't remember those cases happening at all – and I was going to all the courts in that part of the world.

Harry Pugh, born 1934

CHAPTER 7
Growing up

Alvis Evans, aged one, with her brother.

Schooldays at Ross-on-Wye, 1950.

Are the children of today really that different from children in the past? The people of Hereford talk about the games they played, encounters with the law, learning about sex, and designer labels:

Nick Nenadich lost his parents when he was young:

I never saw it in those terms that I was an orphan. We had these three aunties and uncles who we used to rotate around and, typical children, we used to manipulate the situation. If you didn't get what you wanted off one set you'd say, 'They don't look after me' and they'd say, 'Oh there, there, there, come and have a bite to eat' or 'Leave it to me, I'll get that for you'. So it worked to our advantage as well as our

disadvantage. They were immensely kind people, but very different in the sense their children had grown up, they were from another generation and they were entering into another time in their lives when they should have been putting their feet up and doing what they wanted to do – and all of a sudden they had two small boys. Looking back now it must have been very difficult for them. They weren't very affectionate, in the sense they didn't give you a kiss or come and say goodnight. They were hard around the edges but very soft inside. I know they cared but their mechanisms for expressing it were kept under wraps. But as I got older, I often did feel our experiences were very different, and with my own children I've tried to remember that, and made sure there's lots of love and affection for them and lots of holding and hugging, expression of need and being wanted, whereas in my childhood I think that didn't exist.

Nick Nenadich, born 1956

I was a tomboy. I don't think mum ever thought I was going to be a girl … and then all of a sudden I broke out. I must have been about fourteen and we used to spend a lot of time over at my auntie's house with my cousins – and I've got an elder cousin, a girl, she's about four years older and I remember her with the clothes and the make-up and the boyfriend and I thought, 'Oh, that looks interesting'. Following her around – I must have been a real pain. All of a sudden, it must have been overnight, I went from this tomboy into clothes, fashion. Boys [had always been] friends, not boyfriends – I mucked in with them, climbed trees.

Nicki Scott, born 1965

We used to walk about a mile and a half to school. It was a bit hot in the summer and a bit cold in the winter but you did it. There was no other alternative. In the summer we used to cut across the fields but we all ended up rather muddy getting to school. It didn't bother us a great deal. [We didn't go to school much] in 1963, during the first part of the year, because of the snow. It wasn't so important then. It didn't seem to matter if you had time off school.

Gary Starkey, born 1951

Peter Mokler's school outing in Radnorshire, 1932.

Fred Morris and his grandson at lambing time. Fred is approximately ninety years old in this photograph.

Nick's school was more on the lines of a prison!

I hold the school in the highest esteem and it was absolutely instrumental in making me the person that I am today in the sense I have overt confidence and I feel I can converse with anybody about anything at any time – and that's very much attributed to the grounding I had at school. But my initial memories were, 'Oh no, this can't be happening to me'. The culture shock, the brutality of the system, the windows had to be open every day of the year six inches. I've got some memories of lying in bed, my nose so cold I couldn't feel it, and people would try and get dressed under the covers, virtually have to break the ice in the bowl to have a wash. I mean it was unbelievable really when I think about it now. I remember one of the first weeks I was there – [I] was just thirteen – I jumped on the bed to get into it and my bed happened to be next door to the house master's room, so as I jumped on the bed it banged against the wall and I remember him coming, dragging me out of the bed, ripping the buttons off my pyjamas and beating me with a slipper six times. If you reflect back to today's age, that would be child abuse and all hell would be let loose. Power was everything. It was a real environment of power.

Nick Nenadich, born 1956

Fred Morris's memories of growing up go back to the turn of the century:

We had plenty of good clothes and plenty to eat – plenty of fat bacon. We lived on the edge of town when I was a boy, but when we went to Woolley Hall we were four or five miles out. We'd have to walk down to Presteigne or take the pony and trap. It was steep hilly country. We used to have to go through four or five woods to get to school. It was dark when we left in the morning and dark when we came home at night. We had slates to write on to start with, then we got pencils. By the time I left they'd just started two to a desk. Our school was pretty good. It was called a British school.

Fred Morris, born 1896

Although Gary was one of nine children, born in eleven years, she liked her own space:

With nine of us, the older ones had to bear the brunt of it – look after us, and we used to do things to annoy them. I used to sleep with my sister in this three-quarter bed. I had this space thing – I had to have my own space in the bed and I used to keep this pin in the wallpaper and give her a jab every so often if she encroached on my space. I saw mother getting the sheets off [one day] and running her hands along the mattress because Mag had complained there was something sharp sticking in her!

Gary Starkey, born 1951

Ann was brought up on a farm and she and her sisters appropriated the pigsty as their den:

We had a pigsty at the bottom of our garden and we used to paint it out – we had old logs for tables and chairs. I remember playing 'WIs' in there because my mum was president of the WI and we used to get the minutes read and signed, and do all these sorts of things. It was good fun.

Ann Jenkins, born 1939

We used to go down the dump and ferret about there for things, and down to the river. We were never questioned where we went, or why or how. We just carried on going and come back again. We never thought about people being unkind to us – we just carried on.

Gary Starkey, born 1951

At the back of the house was open fields but that was built in the late '50s. It was bad news really because we weren't allowed to play there. There were three ponds … we used to play football and cricket, war games and try and shoot newts with bow and arrows and somebody got an old zinc bath and strapped some planks on it and we'd paddle round the pond! There used to be a rival gang that used to come from afar and you could hear them coming because they had upturned dustbins, beating them as war drums, and then we used to send our champion to meet them. He was like the David and he

Peter Mokler, aged nine.

used to fight their champion and whoever won the fight … then we used to get together and have a game of football.

John Ellis, born 1931

I had a brother who was twelve months older than me so I always played with him, and a cousin who was the bane of my life. I was always second in command of the boys' gang. I didn't play with the girls – I didn't like them because girls pushed prams and did soppy things. I liked climbing trees and scrumping apples. All the nice things in life! … I must have been a sanctimonious little prig because we went down the lanes to pick some apples. Well, I knew that was wicked so I wouldn't do it. So I just held the apples, I didn't pick them – no way – and a police car came along. Now, when I was about eight, police cars were very, very rare and the boys just scattered and there was me with my arms full of apples and the policeman got out of the car and I was just rigid with fright and he walked towards me and he just laughed and he walked away so I promptly dropped the apples and ran. I couldn't do it before. The boys had just left me!

Alvis Evans, born 1927

Alvis's family were better off than some of her contemporaries. She tells the story of the local philanthropist, a reputed millionaire:

We weren't well off, but I never got the impression we were poor.

Alvis Evans as a baby.

Alvis Evans' schooldays, 1939.

Some of the children came to school with no shoes on and I had to take a pair of shoes to give to a child that didn't have any – and I don't know who was most embarrassed – her or me. There was Mr Page, he was a corn merchant in St Nicholas Street. He would stop children in the street and ask for their names and addresses and then he would send them birthday cards with money in and he stopped my friend and I but he didn't ask for my name and address and I was ever so upset – and my mother was upset that I was upset, because the little girl I was with was very poor. Obviously I'd got shoes and decent clothes on … but I was quite offended. He was a real philanthropist. He was renowned for doing it.

Alvis Evans, born 1927

Nicki Scott remembers her first kiss:

This boy asked me to dance and I can remember him kissing me. It was awful! It was the worst thing out! He French kissed me. I didn't know what

73

Cyril Bird in 1928.

French kissing was! I just can remember thinking, 'Oh, this is awful!' and I went straight to the loo and washed my mouth out. I was very innocent. Poor boy, I probably frightened him to death. We'd talk about [sex], 'Oh, they're having sex' but we didn't know what it meant – we hadn't got a clue really. At sixteen then, I was really innocent. I wasn't going to have sex until I was married. Some did, obviously. You could always hear people talking about it and you thought you should be – but were they really? As I look back now they probably weren't, they were probably just bragging about it.

Nicki Scott, born 1965

I was very conscious of sexuality – how a young man should act around a young lady – but I hadn't … experienced it and no one had told me and there wasn't the exposure on the television that there is today. And I often felt very awkward about whether I should hold someone's hand or whether I should kiss her or whatever. It was fun days though because we used to go to youth clubs and we'd just dance. What was important was being in her company – it was so powerful.

I'm sure that nothing has changed over the ages. I think the exposure to what you should do and what you could do is greater because it's hyped up through the media. I'm a great believer that experiences are experienced by everybody. They may interpret them differently but they have the same feelings and the same thought patterns and they check things out in the same way … so I'm sure nothing has changed over the ages. There are lot of people who think like I do and they probably did in 1950 and 1930 and 1920. It's just it probably wasn't vogue to talk about in those days.

Nick Nenadich, born 1956

Jill Southall, in 1946, on holiday.

CHAPTER 8
Getting older

Fred Morris on his 100th birthday.

Herefordshire people discuss the pros and cons of growing old – and discount them!

As headmaster I had to retire because of hearing problems. I could impart information but it became difficult for me in a classroom to gather what every child was saying, and I felt I was beginning to create problems for my teachers. I went to see the gentleman in charge of Hereford & Worcester at our local education office and he was a very compassionate man and he said, 'If you feel you have a problem we will do our utmost to help you'. They sent me to a specialist at Hereford Hospital and he said to me, 'Unless you give up your teaching job you will be stone deaf within a year'. So I was quite upset by that – very much so. I think it's a good thing to make changes in life and to do other things that perhaps you wouldn't have done but it's much nicer if you've got time to collect your thoughts and adjust – which I didn't. I coped because I've got a super wife. She said, 'You've got ability in all sorts of things. You were trained as a cabinetmaker when you were a young man, why don't you try to utilise some of those skills and go back to what you were doing years ago. This will give you a purpose'. And that is what I decided to do.

Alf Jenkins

I always tried to sit by him, then if people are saying something (because he always says he misses the last line of the joke) it'd come to the punchline and he's missed it - I can pass on what I think he should be hearing. One-to-one he's fine, and outside with a group he's fine but when he was in crowds he just couldn't bear it. If we went to a meal at the village hall he hated it.

Ann Jenkins, born 1939

My colleagues ... advised me to go on a management course to start a little business. So I went along to Hereford, this business course began and there were sixteen people there listening and one tutor, and at the end of the first day I came home extremely distressed because the tutor had got the window open and all the traffic was roaring by in Hereford. Hearing aids

Alvis Evans in Tywyn, 1998.

were picking up the traffic more than picking up what his voice was trying to tell me and so I came back and said, 'It's a waste of time. I'm not going anymore'. And then it was suggested I took my wife with me because she would be able to assist. She was at home at the time and she went along with me and we had to introduce ourselves and she said, 'We're Ann and Alf Jenkins and I'm the ears and he's the mouth!' which made everyone laugh and broke the ice and we managed quite well. She gave me a synopsis of what was going on and so we became partners in our little business.

Alf Jenkins

He's always said that even though I've got a quiet voice he could always hear me. We think alike. Today he said, 'I must go and phone…' – and I said the name and he said, 'How did you know that?' And I just knew. When you've lived with someone a long time you can understand them can't you?

Ann Jenkins, born 1939

It just gave us an opportunity to do what we hadn't had the opportunity to do for years and years. When you're very, very busy professionally, you don't even go to your own children's speech days and sports days or anything else. You can't sit down and have a break or a cup of coffee together – you can't have lunch together. So I think the most wonderful thing was to be at home and at eleven o'clock she'd say, 'I'll put the kettle on for a cup of coffee' and it was simple things like that. So in a funny sort of way this last decade Ann and I have done things, been able to do things we'd have loved to have done, but never would have done if I'd have had to continue my professional job. Mind you – I'd have had a jolly good pension if I'd carried on till I was sixty-five!

Alf Jenkins

At an age when most people are retiring Janet Robinson moved to Hereford, from London, to open a new business:

Holidays in north Wales were special to us, so we realised how good it would be to live in the country when it became possible. Mark worked in the computer industry and we felt it wasn't a very good industry to try and grow old in. You often retired and died because you were worn out – and it's not much good waiting for a fat pension if you're not going to be energetic enough to enjoy it. And so we began to think we could establish a holiday guest house of some sort, particularly for people perhaps with a disability or in a wheelchair or something of that sort. We were getting quite excited about it then, in the autumn, our daughter (who had just gone to agricultural college) was killed in a car accident, which obviously filled our minds for a considerable number of months and no way could we have moved anywhere for that first year because we got such a

The Haven, Janet Robinson's business in Hardwicke.

lot of support from our friends and family and neighbours where we were living. I think, perhaps, Nell's death may have well given us the final push to make the move to Hay-on-Wye, and her death helped us have the courage to do it and live life to the full.

Janet Robinson, born 1935

Mark and I were both, in a way, retiring and yet we were both starting a new business – and both things, I believe, according to all women's magazines, are pretty stressful – and they were in a way. We both found out things about each other and ourselves that we didn't like particularly. It's one thing seeing one another till nine o'clock in the morning and then not again till seven at night – and then being together all the time and for about six months we were really quite jockeying for position and sorting ourselves out. And another thing about starting a new business, you've no one to blame – so you blame each other at first until you realise you've just got to get on with it. If you teach in a school as I did, you can blame your head of department, you can certainly blame the government. But when you're running a guest house and the cooking goes wrong, or a shelf falls down, that's your problem and you've got to live with it. We opened for Easter in 1987. We were determined we would do, and we had some friends who were Quakers. One of them phoned and said he'd like to bring their poetry group for Easter, which was going to be six of them. Well, we'd got six bedrooms and although that wasn't very economic to have a single person in each it was a nice way to start - not being too frightening - and one of them was going to come early and in fact as he walked in the front door we were putting up the last picture in the hall. It was as near as that! And we told him not to touch the paint on his bathroom door as it was only almost touch dry. So it was a very near thing. But of course they were very loving and very supportive so it was really like having friends. You never really know what is likely to happen. I mean I'm sixty-three and quite a few of our family say, 'Aren't you going to retire soon? Haven't you been doing this for long enough?' And in the middle of summer when we've perhaps ten guests in and we're cooking dinner for perhaps five nights of the week, we can get a bit tired, and, quite naturally, one does wonder. But at the moment we're quite happy where we are. It would be very difficult to leave the place. Having lived all our lives in streets, to live in a house which has wonderful views of countryside from every window and where you can walk out at night and watch the stars, huge stars, shining and hear the owls and have bats swooping over you – it's going to be quite a wrench. Obviously, we shall have to do

it because it's a large house and not to run a business here would be absurd with just two of us in it. But we have paced ourselves so that we don't do as much work as we used to. We shut, more or less, from November to March, and we do take the odd break in the season as well. And we hope that we shall realise when it's the right time to move on.

Janet Robinson, born 1935

80

CHAPTER 9

Technology

Haymaking in the 1940s with the horse-drawn Bamford mowing machine.

Fred Morris's first home.

Changes in farm life over the century start with Fred Morris, the first tractor, the demise of the horse, and the new ways of making cider. Technology comes to the Herefordshire landscape:

I was born on 5 February 1896 at Presteigne. There were no coolers in those days and milk went warm to the customers. It was three ha'pence a pint. My father was a farmer up in the hills, then we came down to Shobdon, where Sun Valley is now. Everything was done by hand, the horses and everything. You was up early in the morning to get your horses ready for work. We were out at seven in the morning and we worked the horses till eleven, then we brought them home for food, back out at two and in at six at night – and you'd got to see to them after that. There's none of that now. It's a lot better now. You can go out in the morning, press a button and you're away! With luck.

Fred Morris, born 1896

My father bought a Titan tractor. It was a very big tractor. They weren't much use on the land – they were too heavy. They were ... made in America and sent over in the First World War. Some went down with the ship, but some of those were got up again. We had one that had been under the water and it worked alright. We used it for belt work. I think we bought it for £5. I was driving one of those right up to 1943. It was on iron wheels and to go on the road we had to put solid tyres on it. Of course it was only any good on the road. We had to put chains round the wheels to get any form of grip at all [on the turf].

Cyril Bird, born 1921

There had been a lot of changes since my father's day. Now everything has to be tagged and marked and papers to fill up. We'd none of that. Everything has got to be numbered now. I remember the first binder and the first threshing machine coming. We used to do it with the old flails and a bit of threshing and the old reaper (we called him) made sheaves and tied them behind him. It was all done by hand. It was wonderful when the binders came on the scene, and now we've got the combine. My father never had a tractor – he retired before they came in. I never had a tractor till late – it was all horses. We used to breed our own and break them in and during the war they used to come and commandeer your best horses. You'd got nobody to work for you much. They'd fetch horses off you and the next week you'd have notice to plough up another twenty acres – and you'd got no horses and no men to do it with!

Fred Morris, born 1896

We were all allotted our chores, there was so much to do – peeling the vegetables, feeding the hens, mucking the hens out and [as we got older] we got more involved with the big animals. And harvesting of course was always very busy. It was all raking in the hay and turning it over by hand and picking stone was a nightmare. We all had to pick stones. To put the bales up on the loader, they all had to be lifted one by one with a fork and that was jolly hard work, we all had to get involved. [Stone picking] was an awful job. When the plough went through the soil it would turn up a lot of stone and

Fred Morris at Park Farm, Orleton.

Fred Morris and his team.

[they] were a nuisance on the land. They'd get into the machinery so we had to go along with a bucket and pick the stone up – a ten-acre field. Picking stone was a laborious job and we used to hate it.

Gary Starkey, born 1951

There were nine horses on the farm. The main horses were Snip and Lively that did most of the work. Lively was an old plodder and Snip was always dancing about. If you had the two together it was so difficult. I remember an old farm worker called Jim Walker and he drilled eight acres of wheat with these two horses. The one jumping up and down and the one plodding, yet he drilled this eight acres quite straight! The patience they had with the horses. They knew just how to manage them. I had lots of experiences with them really. I had one or two run away with me 'cos

Peter Davies with 'Prince', *c.* 1939.

Jill Southall's father baling hay on an early mobile baler, 1945.

we used to train horses and we had the old horse, Lively, in the shafts, and the young horse in the traces in front trying to pull the cart. The boss said, 'If ever they run away and they get down, you sit on their heads! Because if they can't get their heads up, they can't get up'. And one did run away with me one day with the horses and cart and I got down on his head and I shouted until somebody came!

John Thacker, born 1927

I do remember him [my father] telling me about these farmers – they used to lug the coal for the threshing [machine] from the station. This farmer was lugging the coal on a wagon with two horses from Wooferton Station up to Richard's Castle, and just at Richard's Castle the vicarage is right on a steep pitch, and these horses stopped right outside the vicarage and no amount of coaxing would get them to go again. It wasn't long till the vicar came out to see if he could help. Vicars are very helpful, even if they don't quite know what they're doing! Anyway, they tried to coax and cajole these horses but they couldn't move them. At last the waggoner was getting a bit fed up, it was getting dusk and he wanted to get home. He turned to the vicar and said, 'Vicar, I'd be very pleased if you'd go back in your vicarage, close all the doors and the windows, and then I shall be able to speak to my horses in a language they understand!' A few choice swear words and they were away!

Cyril Bird, born 1921

Peter Davies with his father and Albert Green. They are pictured with the first machine-picked hops.

I remember the grey Fergies coming. That was the innovation to farming because of the hydraulics. We'd never seen that. Something that could lift so easily, whereas before, anything that was lifted, either you cranked it up or you lifted it by hand. You could tip a trailer right up, no problem. You could lift it to a great height, quickly, which meant that the load was off, manure lugging, no problem. Then the first combine came. That was brilliant.

Dave Morris, born 1953

Not everybody took kindly to technology:

There wasn't that many combines about to start, actually, but this farmer, his son wanted to buy this combine and he kept on to his father about buying this combine, and buying this combine and, well of course, he wouldn't agree to buy this combine – he was still cutting the corn and threshing it, like. And at last finally he agreed he'd buy a combine. So he bought this combine and put it in the shed and anyway they started on the harvest and

86

he started with the binder and the son said, 'You gonna use this combine like?' and [the father] said, 'Oh, I agreed to buy the combine. I didn't agree to use it!' So you can tell a lot of these farmers took a lot of persuading. I was threshing right up to 1965, I think it was.

Cyril Bird, born 1921

Hop picking changed entirely:

The next mechanisation was the hop picking machines – they came in 1953. They had one at Dormington, but father was always very reluctant. He could see big improvements taking place in the machines and it wasn't until 1957 we had our first hop picking machine and I could remember going with him, the previous hop picking, to look. There were two type of hop picking machines.

He said to the one manufacturer, 'What about servicing and repairs?' and he said, 'It won't need repairing' and father said to me after, 'Well, I've never seen a machine that doesn't want repairing so we chose the Brough picking machine. I can remember the look of horror on my father's face when he saw the first hops going through because it does look a very brutal action and it was fairly brutal in the early days.

Peter Davies, born 1923

It was taking, in these days, about twenty-five to thirty people to run each hop picking machine. We had two hop picking machines so we had about seventy people instead of three, four, five hundred, so it made a big difference really to the local community because it affected the takings of the local shop,

Peter Davies and the first commercially grown dwarf hops.

the pubs – changed the whole way of life in the countryside at hop picking time. But really it had to change because people by the late '50s weren't wanting to start work at five in the morning and they were starting to come from Hereford at nine o'clock and going back at three o'clock because they had to collect their children from school. We couldn't get enough people. Hop growing as we know it would have ceased and we were soon picking better crops with the machines than the hand pickers could.

Peter Davies, born 1923

Disease control was done with powder. You had nicotine dust to kill aphids, and I actually got nicotine poisoning and I was quite ill from dusting. Then you had sulphur to control pests and copper dust to control mildew. We had the horse-drawn powder machine and we had a super old horse called Tom who pulled the powdering machine with the engine on – and all I had to do was fill the duster up, start the engine up, put it to go, put the horse in the end of the row, run up the next row and meet him at the end of the row and put him into the next row – and we would do that perhaps three or four hours in the night, starting at ten o'clock and go on till two o'clock the next morning. Then, toward the end of the '40s, we changed over to sprays and the new organophosphorus sprays came in for controlling hop damson aphid. And you couldn't put those on with dust so you had new sprayers which were horse drawn, with an engine on to begin with, then

obviously air-assisted fan sprayers came in later.

Peter Davies, born 1923

The chemical age took a hold, but the farmers didn't know what they were dealing with:

Chemicals were a big breakthrough for farming. I think they've also been the downfall of farming. We didn't use rubber gloves, or face masks or shields. You'd get it all over yourself – and of course it was going in your system and you didn't realise what you were doing to yourself. When I was sixteen, we had a sprayer for the first time. I can still taste that spray now from when I used to go round the fields – and that was called Phenoxylene Plus – and I bet anybody who was at work at the same time can tell you what it smells like and tastes like because, the spray – if the wind was blowing towards the tractor, there was no cab – you just sat there and sat in it and went on. We didn't know we were doing wrong.

Dave Morris, born 1953

I remember years ago when a spray called Phenoxylene was eighteen shilling a gallon and you could spray that on almost anything. It would kill the weeds anyway and it was about the only thing I knew about and I used to buy enough for perhaps two or three years – and then when I went back one year and I hadn't got any and I said to the chap, 'I've come for some Phenoxylene spray' and he said, 'How many acres have you got?' And we added it up what I'd got to do and he said, 'You'll want about ten or twelve five-gallon drums' and as were carrying them out I said, 'How much a drum is it then?' I think he said about £40 – and I said, 'You can take most of it back and I'll do it myself and only spread it where I need it!' There'll be a famine if we don't use it – there'll be a famine. Which is the worst I don't know.

Joe Morris, born 1925

Cider making has changed beyond recognition:

If you go right back to the early days of cider making, every other farmhouse around this county had a mill of their own – or if they didn't, there was a chap who was prepared to travel with his mill and make the cider, and it was a means of getting alcohol. Everyone had their own special recipes and if you come and work on the farm you can have all the cider you can drink working there. That was what they used to go for. That old traditional cider they talk about now is a bit of a myth now. A lot of it that you come across that is sold over the farm gate is terrible stuff. It's dreadful. Three-man cider they call it. One to drink it and two to hold him down while he drinks it! And that isn't really acceptable.

Cedric Olive, born 1935

They used to have cider you see, and my father, he didn't care too much about cider and it came to night and

Cyril Bird with a Titan tractor.

he'd got his jar left and he thought, 'I'll take that home. I might have a drop for supper'. He was walking across the field to go home and he met Mr Williams [the farmer] coming down. Of course, he's in trouble now because he's got the cider with him. He said, 'I thought I'd take this drop of cider home, in case …' and Mr Williams said, 'You're doing the right thing, I don't like my men to have too much cider'.

Cyril Bird, born 1921

It used to be a tannic traditional cider. The old cider maker would put sides of beef into his cider. He did that because it made good cider. It added yeast, it added nutrients and it added a fining to clear the cider, good fermentation, quick fermentation to clear the cider. Most of the practices we still use today but we use the scientific principals behind them. Instead of adding beef we add nutrients and we add yeast.

Jonathon Blair, born 1957

I can remember as a schoolboy, both directions, through town, horse and carts, old vans, wheel barrows, with apples on them – queueing up to go into Bulmers. And when I say the queue – from Bulmers in Ryelands Street would stretch from there to Kings Acre Hall – I'm not exaggerating. There was no control on it, you could bring it in when you were ready. All this fruit was supplied by farm orchards, small back garden orchards, all varieties and the whole lot was produced on standard

trees (the standard tree is the tall tree). That's all changed over now and gone to bush orchards.

Cedric Olive, born 1935

The biggest change is we used to get one big, good year and then the following year used to fail. These days we get a good year, and in a bad year we get 90% of a good year. They pick them up now with these great big motor mower-type things – they look like lawn mowers with rubber blades on and they sweep the apples up. It's a mixture between mowing them up and sweeping them up. [It] bruises very easily – a lot of the fruit is grown so it is resistant to bruising and it is also harvested a little earlier than it would be normally, and much more quickly. They *could* harvest in four weeks – if we could process that quickly they would do it, but if you asked the biggest gang of workers to go

Sheep dipping, c. 1931.

Ploughing in 1947.

out into the fields it would take them between September and December just to get all the apples off.

Jonathon Blair, born 1957

It used to be a hands-on job. Now you are sat in front of a screen and you've got a PC there and it's controlled. You just sit there and as long as the programmes are all written correctly – away it goes! There's only one thing they can't do – Mother Nature always has the last say.

Cedric Olive, born 1935

But surely it still tastes the same – or even better?

Fifty years ago everything would be manual. There would have been nothing at all that was automatic. Ninety per cent is in the control room – rather than a person going out to connect between vessels, he just sits in a control room and dials what he wants to move from which vat, presses a control button and it happens. But the control on blending is still exactly the same as it would have been fifty years ago. We still control the blend by manual calculation. The cider making process is still reasonably natural.

Jonathon Blair, born 1957

CHAPTER 10

Eating and drinking

A family picnic.

The grocers shops of the past, sexing an egg, genetically modified food, and family mealtimes all come under scrutiny:

Janet Robinson sets the scene in the traditional grocers shops:

Great-grandfather started the shop and obviously it grew and it moved premises. It was quite a large shop with a 100-foot frontage. When I was a child it had mahogany counters all down one side and behind were wonderful mahogany and glass fitments. And the staff were dressed in crisp white linen overalls and the customers would sit on chairs giving their orders or having them made up on the site – and you realise of course that there is no grocers shop of that kind left. In fact, people don't know what a grocer is.

Janet Robinson, born 1935

By 1951, I think supermarkets were just coming into being and my uncle, who had come back [from the war], he could see the way things were going and we actually turned the shop into a small supermarket. My father came in one night laughing because he'd seen some woman looking round the shelves and had gone up to her and said, 'Excuse me madam, can I help you?' and she'd said, 'Certainly not! I thought it was a serve yourself!' But it was quite, quite different. The assistants found it difficult because … they had been very much involved with the customers – it lost a lot of its interest for them. It's not nearly as much fun filling shelves as actually serving an individual customer and passing the time of day with them. The older people, of course, did need quite a lot of help from the start. They found it very difficult. The younger people liked it because it seemed modern and new.

Janet Robinson, born 1935

Bread was the staple diet, and baker, Jim Franklin, describes the process:

The bread had got to be cheap, good, and got to be well cooked … crusty bread, and it was very important. People would eat a lot of bread. Some farms – we'd drop twenty loaves a week to them but they'd eat it for breakfast, dinner, and tea so it was a most important part of the diet. It was a good, cheap filler for the stomach so you don't need fancy stuff to go with it. In the bakery it was very primitive. The one machine we had from the 1914-18 war, that was a mixer which was taken out into the fields to make the bread for the troops and that was sold off and bought for this bakery. The oven was coke-fired so the dust and the fumes were horrendous from that. Flour was tipped down a chute in the roof, down into the bakery, which covered everything with white dust so that [from] the health and safety aspect of life it was quite horrendous! Very, very basic – but this was the normal bakery of its time

Jim Franklin, born 1940

27th October 1965

Item		£	s	d
2 lb Butter A			7	=
4 lb Sugar			3	=
¾ lb Tea Typhoo.			5	3.
2 Pkts Dried Fruit.			3	7.
3 lb R.R.S.R. Flour.			2	1
1 Vim 3ᴰ 22.			1	1
½ lb Fosces Mints			1	1
Choc	G		4	1
Cheese	G		4	6
Spillers Shapes	G		2	4.
3 Large Pal.			5	10½.
½ lb Bosc Suet.			1	6.
Pay Papers Book 5			3	5.
Jar Gravy Browning H.			2	6.
Tin Stewed Stoke.			4	3.
Honey. 4# G.			3	2.
2 lbs G. Dried. G			3	8.
Crumpets G.				9.
Bananas.			1	6
£		3-	0-	7½

One of Doris Tunley's shopping lists, 1964.

Many people kept their own livestock. Doris Tunley's mother could tell the sex of a chick before it was hatched!

We had chickens. We would go out of a night, looking them over and if you wanted one, if one was lame or anything, well, you'd grab that one and have a look and you killed that one off. A nice fat one. If you picked up a thin one, you'd chuck that one down again, you wouldn't bother. My mum had different rings on them so she knew their age group. Certain colours were certain ages. She reared all her own. If you wanted cockerels she could pick the eggs out and she'd have them on the table with a needle and a long piece of thread – and nobody dared touch the table – and if it went round it's a hen and if it goes back ad forth it's a cockerel. She would sell off sittings of eggs with one cockerel to go with it. If it was a weak one, it didn't swing quickly to go round – she'd put it aside because she'd say it wasn't going to be a strong chicken inside.

There was a pig killed in our family so there was always boiled bacon, and my dad would eat lumps of fat so long as he had mustard and bread. I hated fat. The head and ears was always done up into brawn and mum would get down the well with a cane and you turned all the chitterlings and done them with water. I couldn't do it! I didn't even like them unless it was the little tiny plaited ones. And then the bladder that came out of the pig, that was made a football. It was blown up and it made a good football. Dad liked the trotters … there wasn't a scrap from that pig that was wasted.

Doris Tunley, born 1924

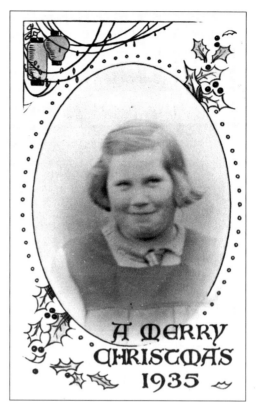

Doris Tunley in 1935.

No fridges, no freezers and no bottled milk:

You'd have your beef delivered on a Thursday to eat on Sunday and you'd no fridge … mum would wash it over with vinegar and it would be perfectly alright. And if you bought some suet from the butchers to make your suet pudding you'd put that down into the bag of flour. The flour kept it fresh. The milk, you had it from the farm. You didn't have any of this bottled milk and I reckon it kept real well. There was nothing concocted. If, in the summer you were worried about it, my mum didn't boil it – she would put a saucepan with water in it, put the milk into a jug, and then put the jug into the

Doris Tunley with her mother and grandmother, 1934.

were basically draught cider, which in them days would be very cheap and a good drink – and it would deliver that alcohol people were looking for. The bottled cider was more served over the bar in the pubs for people with a sweet tooth, and the seasonal variation in the drinking was tremendous. You'd get very low [consumption] in January then you'd come into a hot summer and it would just go off the scale. Now, it's evened out a lot better even if we still get two peaks in the year. The draught cider is a very small volume these days, it's almost insignificant in what we do – if you look at that against the keg cider. We've gone from the wooden barrels to plastic barrels and the cider that is packaged now is looking at the drink trends of the young people. I always think that cider is something that young people wean themselves [from] onto something more. When we were kids you'd always drink the cider first then you'd get more macho and go onto the beer! ... Now there are the designer drinks ... they are all ninety-day wonders ... if you look at alcopops, they've almost died the death now.

Cedric Olive, born 1935

water and it sat on the fire, with a good fire under it. When the milk had got skin on top then it was scalded and it would keep. You've got your own ways of doing all this and keeping it. You couldn't have things on a whim. I brought an ice cream all the way from Ross on my bike and of course, when I got home it was all runny. I brought it home for my mum.

Doris Tunley, born 1924

One mustn't forget the famous Herefordshire cider:

Cider has always been looked at as a rural drink. It wasn't high profile. The large volumes we used to deal with

I think I became vegetarian when I was pregnant with my third child in 1972. I had been moving in that direction. I'd heard a few programmes about factory farming. I remember a particular one about hormone tablets in chicken necks that hadn't dissolved – and you boiled up your chicken necks to make your gravy and got a big blob of hormone tablets – and that Marks & Spencers were the vanguard of not selling

96

chicken who'd been treated that way, and that was way back in the '60s. We've hopefully seen the worst of the processed food, the fast food, high fat, additive, colourant-filled food with all its side effects. I was aware of that back in the '60s … when there was all this stuff about saccharin. And I started being very careful about food from that day on and I must say all these years later, at my age, I look back and I feel very pleased I did because these things do catch up with you.

Kate Henning, born 1944

My current preoccupation is with genetically modified ingredients. If I am going to eat something I want to be able to choose to eat it, therefore it has to be labelled so I could look at the label and say, 'Yes, I understand this has got genetically modified whatever – and I choose to eat it. I've weighed up the risks and I'm happy that it's a small risk … whatever'. What I don't want is to pick up something not knowing. If it's a supermarket that isn't labelling, I don't shop there. I boycott them, and I tell them why and I write with receipts saying, 'You have lost my custom because of this, and I used to spend 'X' and I'm not going to spend it any more'. But it's hard work and you have to write letters and ring customer care. Why do I have to do that? That's the crux of it. Why am I having to go through these hoops in order not to eat something that ought to have been labelled in the first place?

Sarah Blenkinsop, born 1962

I get really pissed off with the amount of food that's thrown away, so we used to go round restaurants, supermarkets, we used to do 'the dreaded' bins! But the amount of food they throw away is unbelievable. Supposedly out-of-date and this sort of thing. We used to get given ridiculous amounts of stuff – cooked hot food. Some restaurants used to say, 'Come in' and they'd lay a table for us. It was a really good time! We weren't begging, we were entertainers and they'd see we had the instruments and we were something a bit different. It made me realise you didn't need money to buy food.

Sam, born 1967

Cedric Olive at the age of eight.

Arthur Morris describes how to keep potatoes in peak condition:

Every workman on the farm had a row of potatoes in the field and if they had another baby they had an extra row in the field – another nipper, another row. They'd grow quite a quantity, maybe getting towards a ton. You couldn't keep them in the house so they'd have to put them in a 'tump' in the garden. You brought the potatoes in bags and they were tipped up on the soil, and then covered with straw and then dug round the outside, quite a trench, and then [you] threw the soil up over and that kept the frost out and the water away from the potatoes so they didn't rot. They'd keep then, with four or six inches of soil over them, as nice as anything. You'd got to watch as you didn't get the rats in. If a rat went in he was quite happy because it was warm in there so if one went in you'd got to trap it. [The potatoes] would keep from October to March. The farmers used to do the same thing with mangols. Of course they don't grow mangols now, but they were very good for the sheep when they were lambing.

Arthur Morris

The cottager's pig and the farm cider:

Everybody kept a pig … and in them days everybody had cider on the farm. A hogshead was 110 gallons and all the farmers made quantities of cider. Some of it was terrible stuff. The pig killing was quite a do … I can remember when we were on the Gatley estate, an old man named Davies, he used to walk everywhere to kill these pigs and he'd come and kill the pig for you. He'd be there in the morning, ten o'clock-time, and you'd got to get the cord on this pig and the bench there, and if you were going to scald him you'd got to have the old furnace for the washing – filled up and get it boiling. But lots of people burnt them. It was less trouble to get them burnt. They'd have to be scraped afterwards, which was quite a lot of bother. You'd run the pig out past the bench then as he come by you'd grab his legs, up onto the bench with him, then you'd slit the throat. You'd got to bleed them and the more they kicked the better because you'd got to get all the blood out. Then [the pig was] burnt or scalded and scraped, then carried into the house and hung up on a hook. Then they'd slit him down and take the belly out. Nothing was wasted on a pig. The old butcher, he'd stop and have some dinner, and some tea. Next day he'd kill somebody else's pig and he'd call by and cut yours up. You wanted a bit of nice frosty weather if you could, then he'd cool well. He might charge six shillings. You might make the meat last for about a year. Every cottage had a pigsty.

Arthur Morris

CHAPTER 11
Playtime

The New Year Round Table Ball, 1957.

Joan Thomas and her sister enjoy the beach.

Saturday night at the movies, knickerbockers and kipper ties, and the lady who got her name up in lights. Herefordshire goes out on the town:

Once a week I would go to the cinema. We used to call it 'the pictures' and it was on from early evening all evening and you could go in at any part of the programme you liked. You didn't have to wait for it to start – it continued and went on and on. So when you were ready you paid your money and you went in. I used to sit down and watch the programme round and round and round, knowing I couldn't get a bus home until ten o'clock. But I always made sure I slipped out before they played 'God Save the King' because they always had to play the national anthem at the end of any public event then, and I daren't be seen walking out during the playing of the national anthem. So I used to leave earlier and go and catch my bus.

Joan Thomas, born 1925

In the evening, there were several of us there who would have a go boxing – we had boxing gloves up there. We had a rifle range. We used to amuse ourselves. We always went to the local dances in the villages around us, but it was a long way to walk! It was morning when you got home – then to work

Fred Morris, born 1896

I remember at the Odeon Cinema, which we called the posh one, if you went there at a certain time for a cup of tea in the restaurant you could be privy to a wedding reception going on at the other end, and if you cocked your ears you could hear the speeches as well. That was lovely. The Ritz (it's now the ABC) was in Commercial Road. During the interval an organ came up through the floor and it changed colour as the man played it and we were all invited to sing songs from a sheet that came down with the words on. Those that weren't licking ice creams could sing. And the other picture house in Berrington Street was called the Palladium – but mostly it was called the fleapit. I think every town has a fleapit!

Joan Thomas, born 1925

During the war, we had such a lovely ballroom at the hostel, that's where we went. Always when we went in there the band was playing and, if they saw a number of land girls (we would be dressed in our dresses – we wouldn't have our uniforms on), they always used to play a thing called the 'Woodchoppers Ball'. And if there were any black yanks there they used to contort as though they were rubber. It was a lovely tune for doing a jive to – and they used to turn themselves inside out and they would grab hold of you and pull you about and swing you round and you couldn't do it but you tried to and you pretended you loved it. In those days you danced with a lot of different people. You didn't always have the same partner and they always

Joan Thomas and her sister, 1945.

Alvis Evans – all dressed up, *c.* 1944.

dances – even at the age of sixteen, seventeen. You made your own clothes, a lot of them. I made a hat out of fox fur and we used to think we were the bee's knees, walking around with our coats and hats on. In the summer, you'd carry a great big portable record player around with you and sit playing Frank Sinatra records which had just come out – as long as my father didn't hear about those either. He didn't approve.

Alvis Evans, born 1927

Nicki Scott recalls the world of high fashion in the 1970s:

I'd got to have this frilly shirt with the laces down the front, and these knickerbockers in cord. I must have looked a real sight! There used to be the discos that they'd have at the Talbot Hotel in Leominster on a Saturday night. We'd go there as a group of girls, putting on extra makeup in the loos (that we weren't allowed to do when we were at home) and my dad had got this thing – even now he goes mad – if I'm not wearing tights in the summer. I can remember even now wearing them to school and the minute I was in the bus taking them off and putting them back on five minutes before I was going home. I'd spend hours up in my bedroom, put the one outfit out, then my friends would phone, 'What are you wearing?' 'I'm wearing a skirt'. 'Oh, I was going to wear trousers'. We'd all end up looking the same by the time we'd finished! And the hair gel! I'd have people over to stay and the LPs would

used to play a thing called a 'Tom Jones' where the ladies just walked round in a circle in one direction and the men walked round a circle in the other direction and you danced with whoever you stopped by. If there was somebody you really liked you used to sort of hesitate and hope the music would stop.

Joan Thomas, born 1925

My favourite outfit was a green skirt with a green bolero. I had one of these *Gone with the Wind* dresses which was a circular dress and of course, as you danced it just floated out! Of course the skirt went on before my father used to meet me from the be going on the stereo and we'd be getting ready together. The gel would go on, the lipstick, the eye shadow – 'Get that off!!' as you were coming down the stairs – so you'd go back up and tame it down but it would all go in the bag with you. Alcohol, smoking – not an issue. We were just really looking forward to going out. There was one girl that was very influential over everybody. She was very tall and slim, almost the head of the gang – [she'd say] 'Let's try smoking!' I can remember going into the loos at the Talbot for a puff on this cigarette. That was enough, I didn't want any more! It was great fun.

Nicki Scott, born 1965

People weren't as free and easy with their sex lives as they are now. Promiscuity wasn't a word, I don't think, in those days. I don't know

Alvis Evans at Barry Island.

Alvis Evans on the River Wye.

Left: John Hurley and Heather, 1961. *Right:* John Hurley and best friend, 1959.

what other people did, I've only got myself to speak for, but I know I almost got engaged to one of my American boyfriends. Almost.

Joan Thomas, born 1925

W
e used to play at Kimbolton Village Hall on a Saturday night, and these American soldiers were stationed here at Berrington and they used to come on up to this dance. Unbeknownst to the other two players, I had this music (it was before the Jitterbug got over here). It was 'In the Mood' – Glenn Miller – and of course I practised on this accordion. One night there was a bit of a break and I went up and played this – and these soldiers went absolutely mad. They

caught hold of these girls and they were throwing them about and they didn't know what had hit them. I had to stop. I thought, 'Someone will get hurt'. And I stopped and then I remember the piano player saying, 'Well, I don't know what that was but it certainly got them going!'

Cyril Bird, born 1921

I went to see Bill Haley and it was the most amazing night of my life. It was electric. People were dancing in the aisles, there were girls sitting next to you, and you were sitting there frigidly wondering what to do – and suddenly they were whipping you out of your seat and dancing round the aisles with total strangers. It was a magical thing.

104

I'll never forget it as long as I live – and Bill Haley is not considered to be a very important figure but for me that night … he was the God. I thought, 'That's it. Liberation. I want to go out there and see the world, go to America, see the home of Rock and Roll!'

John Hurley

Most relationships at college in the '70s were highly sexualised in the sense it would be nothing for somebody to meet somebody on a Friday night and you wouldn't see them till Monday. The male thing is, 'Get yourself all dolled up – we're going to score tonight! I wonder which lucky girl is taking me home!' People would almost have little tick charts:

'How many girls have you been out with this term?' 'I've been out with seven' 'What was she like?' 'Well she's alright – I can recommend her!' Whether that's male bravado … but those reflect the time, as far as I'm concerned, fairly accurately!

Nick Nenadich, born 1956

And the lady who had her name in lights in Ross-on-Wye:

He said he was coming to see me at eight o'clock and I waited in. Eight o'clock – no Henry, ten o'clock – no Henry, and I couldn't believe I'd waited in. My mother said, 'What are you going to do?' and I said, 'I'm going out bopping!' She said, 'You can't! That boy's coming all the way from

Kay Morris on an annual holiday in Porthcawl.

Kay Morris at Skegness holiday camp, June 1948.

Wolverhampton to see you'. I said, 'Well if he comes, tell him I've just gone down the road for a packet of cigarettes for you'. Well, I queued up and I paid my money and I went into the Top Spot, as it was then, and like any young girl I danced and I enjoyed myself and all of a sudden there was a tap on my shoulder and I said, 'If you hang on a moment I'll have a dance with you' and this tap came again and I said, 'I said I'll dance with you in a minute!' and as I looked it was my boyfriend – whoops! ... and I said 'It was about ten to ten when I left ...' and he said, 'Jacqueline, I had a puncture, things do happen'. And the last dance was a smoochie and I thought, 'He's my boyfriend – I'll have this dance with him' and he said, 'I'll buy you this place and put your name in lights' and I thought 'Yeah, yeah, yeah, tell me the old story'. And he said, 'I'm serious, one day this will be yours and your name will be in lights' and he kept to his word. He bought it for me and my name was in lights and that was my proudest day!

Jackie Danter, born 1944

106

CHAPTER 12

Going places

Doris Tunley with her mother and father in 1947.

Horse-drawn vehicles, the first Healey motor car, doing the ton, and the story of the Kington bypass. Herefordians are on the move:

My mother used to drive the pony and take us into Ross in the trap and bring lots of stuff back. And she used to stop at the bottom of Gatsford because there were us two girls and her, and she used to bring sharps back for the pigs and she said it was too much for Dolly to pull us all up Gatsford. So we had to get off and walk, and when we got to the top Dolly had got so as she'd stand still and let us all get in again. So when my dad took off to Ross, just him and the trap bringing nothing back, and when he got to the bottom of Gatsford,

Dolly just stood still, so he wondered what was the matter with her. Soon as he got out, she started to walk and when she got to the top she stood still, and as soon as he got in she started off. So, when he come home he said to my mum what had she been doing with Dolly. She said, 'We haven't been doing anything, we haven't been stopping anywhere – well, only on Gatsford for the girls...' 'Ah' he said, 'That's all I want to know. You've trained her well!'

Doris Tunley, born 1924

We had to walk two miles to school. In summer we could go across the fields and we cut a lot off. And there was kiddies come from everywhere. If we'd gone first [to] Big Meadow Gate (as we called it – it was a five-barred gate) we'd put stones across there. If it was us two we'd put two stones there but if it was Cottons they'd put three there because there were three of them – and if we'd come and find three stones there we knew they'd gone and you just shook the gate and you went on. You'd run like mad then to try to catch them and in very bad weather the teacher would say, 'It's snowing, it's going to come on nasty. Now come on Eyton ones, come on Yatton ones. Go get your coat and you can go home first. The other ones can do the clearing up with the books' – because the ones nearer home, they could go last.

My mum went out one time – we were coming back from Ross. Dad always cracked the whip. You didn't hit the horse with the whip, you just cracked it over their backs. Mum wasn't too good at this and she used to crack it

Peter Mokler, aged twenty.

Doris Tunley's Austin Seven.

out the side of the trap and she one day caught a man's trilby and sent it flying. She didn't stop! It was 'Come on for home!' and we took off. It was rather funny. We had a black dog in later years – he was a crafty little monkey and if it would come on to rain he would get down by our feet, and we'd put a rug over our knees so he was in the dry. But he'd keep our feet warm.

Doris Tunley, born 1924

I had to cycle to school, two miles to get to the bus stop, then five miles to school and then we had to run from the bus stop to the school to get in for assembly because if you didn't get in for assembly they used to say, 'Now where are the Orleton children?' And if some

of you got there and half a dozen were hanging behind it was 'look out'. We used to run to get there in time.

Ann Jenkins, born 1939

Sam is a traveller who spends the whole year on the road:

I travel with a horse and wagon. I live like I do, not necessarily because I want to be horse drawn, but because I feel I can be environmentally sound. I feel the world has become a destructive society and its reason to be has just gone crazy. It's ironic they call things construction sites – I think they are destruction sites.

Sam, born 1967

When we got into Ross there was the railway at the bottom at the mill pond, and mum used to put the pony in there and you would take her out of the trap, but not unharness her, and she'd be put at a manger with feed. There was little kids from Tudorville and they were scruffy, rough little devils, toes out of their shoes and perhaps the bottoms out of their trousers almost, but they would come to mum. They'd got to know her and mum would give them grocery and stuff and they would take it down and they would put it in the trap at the railway and you'd give them a couple of coppers or a bun, whatever they wanted, and they wouldn't pinch a thing. And if she didn't want to put the pony up, we wanted to be quicker, she'd find one of them and they'd hold her. I mean today they would have teased her to death and all sorts, but you could trust them.

Doris Tunley, born 1924

What a lot of people don't realise is the first Healey sports cars were built in Hereford and there were sixty-four of the cars built from 1945 to 1950. Most of them were sold to film stars but Prince Bernard of the Netherlands had one and one of the Andrews sisters had one. These cars were £2,382, which was an awful lot of money when one thinks my wage was £4 a week, as a trainee, I suppose. But one could have bought a brand new Jaguar or Alvis for under £800. But these cars were all hand-built and they were the fastest production cars of the '40s – capable of 104mph. Of course in those days I could never ever have dreamt of owning one. Now I do

Peter Mokler behind the wheel of his Westland Healey, which was made in Hereford in 1950.

Peter Mokler's first sports car, a ten-horsepower BSA Scout, 1953.

own one. It's a superb one, a car I dearly love. I think there are seven still in existence.

Peter Mokler, born 1927

We can't keep going on like this. Fine – cars are part of our lives. I'm not suggesting we should throw away the cars and go back to horses and carts, it's not going to happen, but we've got to be more sensible in our use of cars. I mean, we're polluting our own environment. We all breathe the air that's been polluted. I cried when I saw what they'd done to where I used to walk. There was a nature walk in Aymestrey Wood which was beautiful and there were trees that had grown there since the last ice age and all sorts of wildlife, bluebells, and a marsh – and they'd gone through a third of it, not the bottom third but a middle third – bulldozed a great swathe through it and destroyed it simply so people can get somewhere a few seconds faster on a road that will eventually clog up. Because roads generate their own traffic and clog up anyway, at the cost of £14 million-odd – for that, something that had been there all that time was destroyed.

Sarah Blenkinsop, born 1962

To finish, the story of the Kington bypass:

I went into local government to try to achieve a bypass for Kington. It was at the time when there was only one thoroughfare through the town. You couldn't get an emergency vehicle from one side of the town without going through the centre and we did some trial runs and in the height of summer it was taking over three-quarters of an hour to get from one side of town to the other. [It was] maybe only 200 metres and therefore there was a great deal of anxiety for ambulances and so forth. Because I'd been in the town over a decade and was wanting to be involved, I went into local government to achieve the Kington bypass and I stayed in local government over twenty years. I was town mayor on a couple of occasions, I was chairman of Leominster District Council, and as an Independent [I was] involved in political issues nationally later on. [My role] has been my link with the community – [it] has been a main strand of my life. I founded the history society, the Kington Museum and I think from 1970 onwards, I've been totally involved in this town. Although not a member of the local council now for ten, fifteen years, people still think I am, so the connection is still seemingly there. In this town, which is just over 2,000 strong, you just take ten people and those are the people who generate all the impetus, the initiative. The others are supportive and if you wanted to raise money (for the bypass we had to, for our campaign, and now for the Kington Hospital) the money will roll in at the drop of a hat. But I have noticed that when somebody comes into the community, they are more likely to get the job of chairperson or secretary, or treasurer. The locals will be supportive, but in the background. In the '70s I was called Mr Kington and that brought it home to me that perhaps I was getting too involved and taking too many decisions and that was wrong. [Regarding the bypass issues,] in the summer you just couldn't move in the centre of the town. It wasn't doing trade any good because you just weren't safe on the pavements. So much so that seventeen shops were vacant and in a town of this size that was a very high proportion. In the winter it was just dead and people were straying to do their shopping in Hay-on-Wye, Leominster and Hereford. Now, more people are coming to town to shop. Initially there was opposition from the local council. There was a scheme for making an internal road by making a huge gap within the main street and taking down half of another street to make a wide through-road and I was opposed to that because the character of the town would have been greatly affected. And I was elected chairperson of the council and because of my interest in the bypass and I had to draw out the actual meeting so one or two of the people who would have opposed the actual bypass left, then I put the motion forward that the town council should support, so it was initially an upward struggle – but the majority wanted a bypass. So much so that we put it to the electorate when there were six seats vacant on the town council. All six put up as a block – 'The Bypass Six' – and all six were elected. So the town rallied but some of those in authority were dubious about the benefit. When we said we wanted a bypass, it was in the early years of the amalgamation of Herefordshire and Worcestershire, and Kington was joint-tenth with Broadway for a bypass and yet it was the first to be implemented. So, you can see it was a battle, but we achieved it. I can remember going to Worcester – we all had a ten-minute slot to talk about our own bypass so they started with Hereford bypass and so forth and all the way down to ours, and we were eleventh because Broadway spoke before us because they were alphabetically above us. And everybody spoke more than ten minutes, and everybody was dead, they were tired, they were sleeping, fed up of all this so the only thing I did was to go up to the platform, ask the chairman to get up off his feet and turn the chair round, then took three strides and asked for another chair to be placed where I stopped and I said, 'That is the width of our Duke Street, which is one of our four principal streets'. And I said, 'If we are competing with Broadway – you put one of their plane trees, and it would actually fill the street, we wouldn't have enough room between the buildings'. And I said, 'I appreciate that not many of you here in Worcester know where Kington is. Could you please just wait a moment' and I walked to the end of the hall, took the plan of the bypass down, rolled it up, and as I came past the planner, I put it on the desk and I went back to the platform and said, 'Next time I'm here in Worcester, would you please do me the privilege of having the map of Kington the right way up!' And I just left. There was silence. And we got the bypass. They knew where Kington was after that!

Alan Lloyd, born 1936

CHAPTER 13
Life and death

Ann Stokes in her deputy matron's
uniform, 1960.

The staff of the Cottage Hospital in Ledbury, 1955.

Ann Stokes (née Whiting) looks back on the archaic attitude to visiting sick children:

If a child had to be admitted it would be forcibly removed from its mother at the ward door and that would be the last she'd see of it until she came to bring it home. Visits were allowed on a Sunday if the child had been good. But if the child created or screamed when mother left then mother was not allowed to visit. At the time I thought it was barbaric and I said so and I was told, 'But Nurse Whiting, that's the way things are done at the children's hospital. Parents are a nuisance, parents cause trouble. They make the child cry'. A lot of these parents were early twenties or thirties. They had possibly seen their younger brothers and sisters evacuated and been evacuated themselves. They weren't going to let their kids go. They didn't want to let them go. They knew it was the rules of the hospital. Sometimes I think it's gone a bit too far the other way now. There are times when I think a child is getting better, and will do without mum.

Ann Stokes, born 1934

Tuberculosis was rife and many children did not survive. Here is the riveting story of a mother and daughter, Clara Webb and Rosemary Brown, and their life-and-death brush with the disease when Rosemary was five years old:

The earliest memory was being in hospital at the County Hospital and I was up, looking down and thinking how

115

frightened I was to be there and no one coming to me. I remember crying and sitting in bed.

Rosemary

She was X-rayed and he told me straight away she'd got Millery TB. I was shocked – I couldn't get over it. I said, 'What is Millery TB?' and he said 'It's not patches on the lung – it's spots and there's no cure'. That's that. She'd never been parted from me at all. And I just left her there.

Clara

I remember the stark white sheets, the very formalness of the nurses. It was very cold and clinical. There was no love. It was very austere. It isn't like children's hospital now.

Rosemary

I used to go to the hospital very often and ask if I could see somebody or ask about her and they'd say, 'She's alright. She's comfortable'. Then I had a letter from the hospital to say they were sending her up to Nieuport Sanatorium – up at Almeley.

Clara

I came to Nieuport in 1947. In fifty-one years I've never been back. There was a big courtyard, a big house. I remember the ambulance coming through and parking in this square courtyard. I remember the stables. They were open to the world.

There were no doors and no windows and no security obviously. I remember being very frightened. The bed looked out. I remember it vividly – the single bedstead with the iron back and the metal potty under the bed. I remember being very frightened of the wood. I was about seven. There wasn't a door that would shut and the windows were glassless.

Rosemary

All the adults who had TB were over in the big house but over in the stable block were the children. It was round a big quadrangle and all the little bedrooms on wards were round this quadrangle. Some had two beds in, some had four. They took me in to see her – we were both disgusted. We were shocked. She didn't look at all cared for. She got sores on her body. Her hair hadn't been done for days I don't think.

Clara

They just saw to your basic needs. I remember my mother found me very dirty. They didn't bother too much. My hair was unkempt. I was just generally very ill. Abandoned. She came and found me like that and she was so upset she went back and told our local family doctor he was to bring me home. I was to be brought home and if I was going to die I was to die at home in comfort, not in squalor – which it was. He obviously took notice of her and he asked or found out from someone where he could do something for my mother.

Rosemary

116

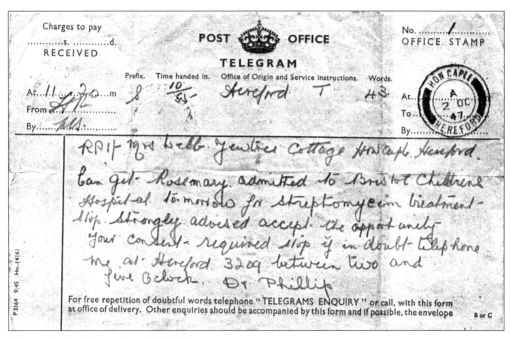

A copy of the telegram from Dr Phillips.

Rosemary Brown revisits Nieuport House in 1999.

Nieuport House, 1999.

A telegram arrived:

2 October 1947:
Can get Rosemary admitted to Bristol
Children's Hospital tomorrow for
Streptomycin treatment
STOP
Strongly advise accept the opportunity
STOP
Your consent required
STOP
Dr Phillip.

The Americans had given the British,
as a goodwill gesture, the funding for
eighteen children to have Streptomycin
treatment, which was a new wonder drug
– untried. And a child had died in Bristol
and I could have the treatment. I
remember being got out of the ambulance
and being carried up the steps at Bristol
and the ambulance man carried me. No
stretchers, no chairs. He just carried me in
his arms in a blanket and he said, 'It's such
a pretty little thing, it's a pity she won't
come out'. And I can remember those
words.

Rosemary

The doctor asked me a lot of questions.
It was a lady doctor. She said if
anything should happen to Rosemary, and
Rosemary should die, 'Would you be
willing to have a post-mortem?' Well what
do you say? You just nod your head I
suppose.

Clara

I was put in Ward 5, which I can visualise
very, very vividly now – outside – on a
veranda. Five or six beds all with red
blankets over them and then at night they
brought us a waterproof to cover the beds

118

A view of Nieuport House showing Rosemary's room.

The interior of Nieuport House, 1999.

A press cutting for the sale of Nieuport House in 1999.

because in the morning you'd probably end up with a pond at the bottom of the bed – or snow, because it was outside. One side was against the back wall and three of the sides were exposed to the elements, not protected in any way by grills or bars, just a low fence at the front. Quite a bit after I was there, they wired up the front and I believe a child was snatched from the next ward across.

Rosemary

People weren't very charitable about TB. You could have had the plague for what they thought about it. It was a terrible thing. It was almost as if you were a leper. That's how you were treated. One person said, 'Of course there has never been anything like that in my family'. But you never know, do you.

Clara

I went down on the train and up to the hospital with the clothes. And to see her walking down the ward all dressed, when in the beginning I saw her carried into the ward – and she never looked back.

Rosemary Brown, born 1941, and Clara Webb

Doctors were not quite the part of the caring profession then:

I remember one instance when they used to sit me on the side of the bed – and my leg went all black – you know. They mightn't look at you for weeks. This morning he looked and he said, 'If it t'inna better in a fortnight we shall have to have it off'. It was three weeks before he looked again. He just nodded and that was that. I've still got me leg – and I'm fit as a fiddle!

Bert Venty

120

Joan Thomas and her twin sister, 1925.

It's not a criticism, but my parents would perhaps sidestep – sexual issues, illness, death were covered up a bit more, and I tend not to. I find being honest with my children quite important and when they ask me questions I tend to answer them. I thought babies came from the Queen! She selected us, and sent us off to our mothers. I thought that until I was about six, but my kids know where babies come from and to a lesser degree how they get there but I don't think you have to be graphic. I think you can tell your kids things in a story-like way where it doesn't sound too bad for them.

Lynne Hunter, born 1959

What you saw in the '70s was there was big money being invested in equipment, foetal heart monitors, and then there was a need to validate that expenditure. There was a lot of pressure going right down the line that everybody had to be in hospital using that equipment, and women lost the plot. They let it happen to them. And when I was pregnant with my fourth child I went through the motions and had a very nice GP and he said home births were just a no-no here and he said, 'I don't understand why they make this fuss but the obstetrician had decreed there must be no home births'. So I had in the back of my mind, 'Yes, I would go to France and have my baby in France'.

Kate Henning, born 1944

I was one of identical twins. We were premature babies – [I was] three and a half pounds at birth and my sister was four pounds. We were seven-and-a-half-month babies. Soon it was discovered there was something wrong with me. I was found I had Pyloric Stenosis, which in lay terms means that the food tube is closed and squashed up so the food couldn't get through. This was a very serious thing and in those days they had no cure for it, until in London some experimental operations had been done and one of them was successful. The operation was called the Ramstead operation. … my mother and father were in a dilemma so they allowed me to go to the Royal Hospital in Wolverhampton at the age of six weeks to have the operation done. They scraped the barrel to be able to pay for it … everything had to be paid for. It was found to be successful … I begun to put on a little weight … but I couldn't have very rich food but the family practitioner hit on the idea of having the cows in the area tested [for suitability] and I had a cow that suited me – and she was my cow and I had milk from this cow only! There weren't any special baby-care units, and no intensive care, and very little specialised care. Hospitals were extremely general. When I came home, my parents still had a very sick baby on their hands, and another one [the twin] she was also premature, so my mother had, with no telephone, no electricity, no hot water, no inside toilet, to look after two very weak babies who needed nappies every day. We only had a coal fire. My father was often away because he was in the police force and often had night duty to do.

Joan Thomas, born 1925

Joan Thomas and her twin, posing in the 1920s.

CHAPTER 14
Beliefs and fears

Holy Trinity Church in Hardwicke. The church's foundation stone was laid in 1849, and it was consecrated in 1853.

From Pagans to Quakers, from walking over hot coals to Church of England schools. People in Hereford look deeply into their religious convictions:

A lot of people I've come across who have got religious beliefs insist that you believe the same thing and I've had a few friends who've become born-again Christians. If that's their choice, fair enough but one of my friends that I made at sixth form did this and he'd actually been quite scared to tell me. Apparently he'd got baptised and he wasn't sure whether to tell me because he thought I'd stop being his friend and I said, 'Don't be so ridiculous. It's not going to happen'. But he had been told when he got baptised that he couldn't be friends with non-Christians and I've come across that a few times since, especially at university and there were people I was coming across who'd been told, 'You can't have a relationship with someone who is not a Christian. You can't have friends who aren't Christians'. I thought it was the most non-Christian thing that anyone could ever say. You have to choose your friends from your religion, not anyone else and I think that's just appalling. I'm not religious still and I don't think I ever will be. I would say I had become more spiritual in the last couple of years, partly through training as an aromatherapist and training in complementary medicine so I've just been shown there is an alternative to being very staunchly atheist. I think it's just being more open to the fact there are other ways of thinking about things. Maybe destiny is taking a hand sometimes. For about the last five years of my life there seem to have been a lot of coincidences when one decision has been followed by another one and everything seems to have gone in a path. I had my life nicely planned out. I knew exactly what I wanted to do and that was it and suddenly everything seems to have been veering off to one side and I'm going somewhere completely different. The atheist side of me says, 'No, no it's just coincidence. Nothing more to it than that'. The other side is thinking, 'Well, I've met a lot of people in the last few years who have got a lot of different beliefs. They do crystal healing or they are into yoga, into meditation or something and I seem to be meeting people who have some sort of belief … and it's almost like I'm being forced to accept there's another way. It might not be the way that I end up taking but it's there if I wish to. I've started doing yoga myself recently and some of my friends think this is the most stupid thing… even ten years ago it was still fairly unusual. Now, just about everyone does yoga. It's quite common. Certainly nothing weird about it but I think if my mother, when she was my age, had said, 'I want to do yoga,' everyone would have laughed at her. And certainly my grandmother – it just wasn't done and I don't think they've had anywhere near the choices I've had. I think that's quite remarkable really because it's not that long – my mum is twenty-six years older than me. She's only twice my age and yet the difference between what I can choose to do and what she can choose to do is just incredible.

Helen Winterbottom-Pope, born 1972

Sam is a traveller. She subscribes more to the Pagan philosophy than the Christian beliefs:

I've always been a bit fervent about my anti-patriarchal religion. The basis of lots of religions is just our natural understanding of respect and peace and love. Jesus had love in one hand and everyone sees that as a good Christian, but historically – he had a sword in the other. Those kinds of 'God' religions have been about war and domination and I see them as being quite destructive. They are also about separation, separating the head from the body – it's all mind from matter. All the male God deities have been about 'separate yourself from the earth' – it's going to be better in heaven. My belief is what keeps me earthed – it's the 'Great Spirit'. It might be male, female, whatever. But it's the Great Spirit, or the Great Spirits and they are not a deity or god – they just are – the Earth spirits. I can't celebrate Christmas, it means absolutely nothing to me and all the Christian celebrations are taken from pre-Pagan ones. Solstice, Easter – Easter comes from the Goddess Oestra – it's about fertility. Solstice is a physical happening, the longest day and the shortest night.

Sam, born 1967

Peter Faulkner dabbled briefly in Pagan values:

I think [being a Pagan] came about by getting heavily involved with Richard Jefferies' writings. He was something of a mystic and a visionary. His idea of the deity and something that was far greater and beyond that fascinated me. I didn't physically worship the sun, or anything like that. I didn't join any cults. But I became separated from conventional religion. There is this wonderment with the natural world and of course the religious people will tell you that the natural world is God's creation. They always have an answer to bring you back in line. Now I'm the local secretary of the Methodist Church in Leintwardine so I have a sort of respectability there but I still very much question, or try to work out, what it's all about and I do have a standard answer to people who say they 'don't believe in God' – [I say] 'The human being isn't intelligent enough not to believe in something which is greater than us'. If you start talking about infinity and the cosmos and light years, which are way beyond us, it's difficult, impossible for us to grapple with that. And if you can't grapple with that then I think it's almost irresponsible to think that there isn't something. Not necessarily a man sat on a throne somewhere. I think that's a bit archaic. As I've got older I suppose I've become more 'respectable!' Going on a tour of the various [world] religions, we're all worshipping the same God under different umbrellas and if mankind could get that one under their belt a lot of problems would be solved.

Peter Faulkner, born 1942

I started life as a member of the Church of England. I was brought up in that church. Initially my beliefs were fairly conventional although I've always been a little bit of a heretic. I could never swallow a lot of things. I would really regard my religious life as one of sort of shedding things rather than picking them up. I feel the rock on which I stand has got a good deal smaller but a great deal more solid. I'm probably one who does believe … there should be nothing between a person and their own God. I can't take too many beliefs at face value. I think I've got to test them out. I think I've done that but I've never been as good in practice as I am in theory. It's a great deal easier to read about forgiveness than to do it! I've been very interested in the Ecumenical Church. I don't believe any one church has a monopoly on God, or any one religion for that matter. A Muslim, a Hindu or a Christian can have equal access to God. It's just they go about it a different way. In adult life, when I was in my forties I was a member of our Parochial Church Council and did quite a lot, in quite a forward-looking church – but I was gradually getting more disillusioned with the church. They didn't seem to be making much progress in getting women into the ministry, or into getting closer links with other churches. We decided to turn to the Quakers and we started going there in the 1980s and found that very much more suited to us. The older I get (although no one would think so, the amount I talk) almost the less one talks about religion – and the more silence one has, the more deeply one can attune oneself to that of the God which is inside you.

Janet Robinson, born 1935

My mum and dad were publicans and you read in *The Bible* about publicans being sinners and I just took it at face value and I thought, 'This is terrible, my mum and dad aren't sinners!' They went to church on a very regular basis and took us to church from when we were tiny. And that gave us a pattern, gave us a moral code. It was inculcated into us to think about other people and what the Ten Commandments meant and should mean and so we were lucky because we were given a basis and I think that's stood me in good stead ever since. One of the problems that youngsters are facing now is they have no specific direction. It's a mishmash of everything and they finish up with nothing. I was a headteacher of Church of England schools for over twenty years and prior to that I was an assistant in Church of England schools. I felt we had got a better opportunity of inculcating some semblance of standard and moral code into those children, whereas other schools that were general schools didn't quite have the emphasis, didn't quite have the backing of the governors … so it was important to me to be in Church of England schools. I made that conscious choice.

Alf Jenkins

To finish, Caius Hawkins expresses his belief in the power within and the self-motivation aspects of the person:

It was an Anthony Robins seminar – he coached the last two American presidents – he's probably the world's most greatest motivational speaker. [I went to this seminar at the NEC] and suddenly this enormous guy comes on stage – about seven-foot tall! This is Tony Robins. There were probably about 1,000 people at this seminar but this guy just filled the whole place. It was like a roller-coaster ride and it was called 'Unleash the Power Within'. It was about finding out the things that block you in life. We all have values and the trouble is these values conflict with what we do and our beliefs. So what we do, we have to prioritise your values, so you are not in conflict with yourself. For example, the concept that having money makes you a bad person [and that] you have to be a bad person to have money. If you have that value – and you need money to survive – then you are going to spend a lot of time feeling bad about yourself or about not having money. So you need to polarise those values so you are not in conflict with yourself. The course is about ... overcoming fear which is a big block. Within a few hours we were being led outside to this enormous bonfire and we all walked across these hot coals – and all came back inside! That was quite a moving experience ... I came away from the course and came away very motivated.

Caius Hawkins, born 1965